CAMBRIDGE

SECOND EDITION

STUDY *speaking*

A course in spoken English for academic purposes

Kenneth Anderson
Joan Maclean
Tony Lynch

CAMBRIDGE
UNIVERSITY PRESS

CAMBRIDGE UNIVERSITY PRESS
Cambridge, New York, Melbourne, Madrid, Cape Town, Singapore, São Paulo

Cambridge University Press
The Edinburgh Building, Cambridge CB2 8RU, UK

www.cambridge.org
Information on this title: www.cambridge.org/9780521533966

© Cambridge University Press 2004

This publication is in copyright. Subject to statutory exception
and to the provisions of relevant collective licensing agreements,
no reproduction of any part may take place without the written
permission of Cambridge University Press.

First published 1992
Second edition 2004
3rd printing 2007

Printed in the United Kingdom at the University Press, Cambridge

A catalogue record for this publication is available from the British Library

ISBN 978-0-521-53396-6 paperback

The authors and publishers are grateful for permission to use the copyright materials
appearing in this book, as indicated in the sources and acknowledgements throughout.
If there are errors or omissions the publishers would be pleased to hear and to make
the appropriate correction in future reprints.

Contents

TEACHER'S GUIDE

References   223

To the Student

Who is the course for?

Study Speaking has been written for people who need to speak English in connection with their academic work. It is intended, in particular, for use on language programmes preparing learners of English for study at university or college.

What does the course cover?

As the *Course Map* shows, the book is in four parts, each of which focuses on different aspects of speaking.

Part 1 features a series of Scenarios. A scenario is a situation in which you need to use English to resolve a problem of the sort that university students face. In each case the scenario involves a conversation (negotiation) between a student and a member of the university staff. Some scenarios deal with problems at the start of a student's university course, such as finding accommodation and arranging English language classes. Others involve issues that students encounter later in their course – for example, essay deadlines and project marks (grades). Scenarios focus on the *flexibility* with which you react in situations where you need to persuade someone to accept your view.

Part 2 contains eight units on topics of current interest such as work, culture and globalisation. Each unit is divided into *Discussion skills* and *Presentation skills*. The work on *Discussion skills* helps you to contribute more effectively to university classes involving tutorials and group discussions. The *Presentation skills* activities practise the necessary elements of successful presentation. The work includes listening to extracts from presentations and analysing them.

Part 3 of the book, *Class seminars*, provides guidance and help on preparing an individual seminar. In the seminar, you give a presentation to your class and then deal with questions and points of discussion from the audience. An important aspect of this part of the course is the detailed evaluation and feedback on your presentation from the other participants as well as the teacher.

Part 4 suggests ways in which you can continue to improve your speaking after the course.

How does the course work?

The speaking tasks in parts 1–3 of the book involve three elements: preparation, performance and feedback. We have designed the tasks to make you *think* as well as speak and listen. Becoming a more effective communicator is not simply a matter of practising the spoken language; practice certainly helps, but the real improvements come from planning *how* to approach a speaking task and evaluating *how well* you spoke.

Kenneth Anderson
Joan Maclean
Tony Lynch

Edinburgh January 2004

To the Teacher

If you have used the original edition of *Study Speaking*, you will see three main changes in the design of the new edition.

1 The *Scenarios* now come first, as Part 1 of the book. The key function of the scenarios is to exploit situations that academic English learners are likely to encounter in their lives as students. The scenarios deal with issues arising at university or college and can be used separately from the global topics covered in the rest of the book. The Part 1 scenarios can be used separately from Parts 2 and 3, in any of the following ways.

   • They can be worked through *before* the class moves on to Part 2. This is how we use them on our pre-sessional course at Edinburgh; the more informal practice they provide helps develop students' confidence at the start of their studies.

   • They can be used *in parallel* with Part 2, so that the problem–resolution practice they provide is interwoven with work on the discussion and presentation skills.

   • They can be used as a *self-contained set* of eight units with a focus on interactive negotiation and problem resolution.

2 The *Seminar skills* component in the original edition has now been divided and extended into separate strands of *Discussion skills* and *Presentation skills* (Part 2). The two elements of each unit in Part 2 focus on one skill aspect but are thematically linked; in Unit 1, for instance, both the *Discussion skills* and *Presentation skills* materials deal with the theme of Work.

3 Part 3, *Class seminars*, is a more comprehensive version of what we called *Extension work* in the first edition. It now provides step-by-step guidance – including checklists of points to keep in mind – to help students plan, rehearse, deliver and evaluate individual seminars. Each seminar includes a presentation to the class followed by questions from the audience and discussion. In this way, Part 3 brings together the discussion and presentation skills that have been focused on separately in Part 2.

Feedback

Another aspect of the new edition is a wider variety of feedback. Since writing the first edition we have experimented with a range of classroom techniques in our EAP (English for Academic Purposes) speaking classes, reflecting recent research into 'noticing' in language learning. The feedback guidance we provide is tailored to the different genres of speaking practised in the book: 'proof-listening' and student-produced transcripts for the *Scenarios*, speaking logs for *Discussion skills*, and evaluation forms for the *Class seminars*. For details, see the *Teacher's guide* (pages 139–201).

Aims

Study Speaking is designed to improve students' speaking skills in English by:

- activating and extending their linguistic competence
- increasing their confidence in using spoken English
- developing their ability to analyse and evaluate spoken performance
- sharpening their strategic competence in face-to-face interaction.

The book has been designed to push the learners to produce the 'comprehensible output' that Swain (1985) has argued is essential to progress in a foreign language. The tasks provide springboards to interaction by challenging the learners' linguistic and cognitive resources. Having planned how to resolve the communicative problem, they perform the task and afterwards analyse how well they coped and discuss alternative strategies.

We want language learners to realise that there is usually more than one possible route to any communicative goal and that success can depend as much on knowing how to approach a problem as on knowing what to say. So *Study Speaking* aims to improve the *quality* of their speaking skills as well as to increase the *quantity* of their knowledge of the language system.

We attach particular importance to getting learners to evaluate their own performances, rather than to rely solely on assessment and correction from the teacher. Studies of the role of consciousness-raising, such as Sharwood Smith (1981) and Rutherford (1987), suggest that as long as the teacher retains the dominant role in evaluating classroom performance, students may not engage in the active self-monitoring that can lead to more skilled performance.

We have not designed the materials to match the specific format of the IELTS test. However, we have indicated with an IELTS symbol IELTS where we believe our classroom tasks practise skills required in the IELTS Interview module.

Rationale

Study Speaking has been influenced by the findings of research into the relationship between classroom communication practice and overall progress in the foreign language. In brief, the relevant findings are as follows.

1 Learning a foreign language requires access to comprehensible input (Krashen 1981). In conversation, difficult input may be made comprehensible through the mutual efforts of speaker and listener to make appropriate adjustments to the interaction. Skill

in making such adjustments forms part of 'strategic competence' in the language (Canale and Swain 1980).

2 That makes it not just inevitable but necessary that learners should encounter comprehension problems, in order to make progress by resolving them. Conversation offers the potential for the development of knowledge of and about the target language, as well as skills in problem solving (Faerch and Kasper 1986).

3 Different types of classroom task make different linguistic and strategic demands on learners. On 'divergent' tasks, such as the Scenarios and some Discussion tasks, where learners do not share a common goal, they tend to produce fewer but longer speaking turns than on 'convergent' tasks such as information gap, which can lead to minimal speaking turns (Duff 1986; Seedhouse 1999). Courses in speaking skills need to provide practice in coping with divergent talk.

4 There are different dimensions of 'success' on a communicative task. For example, a learner's use of interactional strategies should be judged by their effectiveness in getting the message across, rather than by the accuracy of their form (Tarone and Yule 1989). Post-task evaluation should focus on the aspect of performance that is relevant to the skill being practised.

5 Task recycling can play an important role in developing students' language and in their ability to 'notice' the language they are using (Lynch and Maclean 2001). Doing a task again with a different partner can help students to free up spare attention for monitoring their performance. If courses rely solely on practice in one-off communicative tasks, there is a risk that students will gain less than if they are given the chance to refine their speaking performance in a new task cycle.

Design

With these principles in mind, we have designed *Study Speaking* to create opportunities for learners to experience three different sorts of communicative challenge.

Part 1 *Scenarios*

Scenarios involve a situation where two people, such as student and supervisor, have different personal goals and where each tries to get their own way (Di Pietro 1987). The potential for confrontation results in interaction that reflects the unpredictability of such conversation. *Scenarios* provide experience in activities that require a flexible response under social pressure – a type that is often missing from the language classroom (Bygate 1988).

Part 2 *Discussion skills* and *Presentation skills*

Research into postgraduate seminars (Lynch and Anderson 1991) has highlighted specific aspects of group discussion in which international students seem to have considerable difficulty, such as focused questioning and disagreement with the previous speaker. The source of these problems can be cultural or linguistic, or both; whatever the source, the *Discussion skills* tasks will give learners experience of, and confidence in, the give-and-take of academic discussion. The *Presentation skills* work complements the interactive focus of *Discussion skills* by highlighting in turn the key elements of effective presentation, which students can consciously factor into their planning of short talks and papers.

Part 3 *Class seminars*

The final part brings together the skills practised in Parts 1 and 2. Each student plans and delivers a presentation to the whole class, after which they have to handle questions and points raised for discussion by their audience. This combines the skills of preparation and delivery practised in *Presentation skills*, the use of appropriate expressions from *Discussion skills*, and the resolution of unforeseen problems like those arising in the *Scenarios.*

Grading

Although the three main parts of the book are free-standing and can be used in different sequences (see page 7), the reason for presenting them as Parts 1, 2 and 3 is that progress through the course is graded in terms of *communicative responsibility*, that is the degree to which the speaker exercises control over the selection of information. In Part 1, the basic information is 'ready to use' in the form of the Role A and B instructions. The learners work in small groups, sharing the responsibility for working out possible conversational moves and countermoves in advance before they play the scenario. In Part 2, the students have to make selective use of the reading input in order to contribute to discussion of the unit topic, and to plan and deliver short presentations within that topic framework.

   The class seminars in Part 3 then require the students to take on more responsibility – gathering and organising the materials and data for their presentation, preparing visual aids and rehearsing. The presenters are responsible for both the content and the form of their presentation, and the audience for selecting points for questions and discussion.

Timing

Different teachers have different amounts of time available for speaking skills work in EAP courses, so we have included in the *Teacher's guide* some alternative or additional procedures for expanding the activities in the book to suit the time you have available. In their basic form, **Parts 1** and **2** together provide enough material for at least **36 class hours**: 12 hours for the *Scenarios*, and 24 hours for Part 2 (3 hours for each unit's work on *Discussion skills* and *Presentation skills*).

Part 3 is open-ended, with cycles of work allowing each student to plan and deliver at least one seminar. If you have a class of 12 students, then the basic cycle of work comprises a minimum of 6 class hours – with each student getting 30 minutes' time for their seminar (10 minutes for the presentation, 10 minutes for questions and discussion, and 10 minutes for evaluation and feedback). There can of course be as many successive cycles as your teaching programme allows.

The materials for **Part 4** are intended for a single end-of-course session of 60–90 minutes. The session helps students to identify ways of continuing to improve their spoken English after completing *Study Speaking*.

Level

We have found that the materials are best suited to students whose proficiency level is between intermediate and early advanced (approximately IELTS 5.0–7.0, TOEFL 500–600, or CBT-TOEFL 173–250). This is based on our experience with pre-sessional students in Edinburgh and on that of teachers piloting *Study Speaking* elsewhere.

If you have students at higher levels than IELTS 7.0 (TOEFL 600 or CBT-TOEFL 250), then you could by-pass Part 2 and go straight to the Part 3 seminars.

Teacher's guide

The *Teacher's guide* (page 139 onwards) offers separate sections on *Scenarios*, *Discussion skills*, *Presentation skills* and the *Class seminars*. For Parts 1 and 2, each section contains introductory *Background notes* on the design and rationale of the materials, and then *Teaching notes* on the individual scenario or unit. For Parts 3 and 4 there are *Teaching notes*. Finally, there are two sections of *Transcripts*: one containing seven *Presentation skills* extracts; and the other, two sample performances of one of the *Scenarios*.

Cassette/CD

Side 1 of the cassette accompanying this book contains the listening materials for the *Presentation skills* work in Units 1–8. Side 2 contains *Sample performances* of the 'essay deadline' scenario (Scenario 4). The first was recorded by two British native speakers and the second by two international students at Edinburgh. Transcripts of the recordings are provided in the *Teacher's guide*, together with comments on the points we would draw students' attention to in the two performances. However, we would like to stress that these are *samples*, not models; they are meant to give you and your students a basis for comparison with their own performances.

The recordings are also available on CD.

Course Map

Part 1	Scenarios	
1	Language centre	
2	Library	
3	Finding accommodation	
4	Deadline for an essay	
5	Examination results	
6	Changing accommodation	
7	Project results	
8	Research proposal	
Part 2	**Discussion skills**	**Presentation skills**
1	Giving your opinion	Structuring your presentation
2	Agreeing and disagreeing	Speaking in an appropriate style
3	Explaining	Delivery: emphasis and phrasing
4	Making suggestions	Using visual aids
5	Interrupting	Introducing your presentation
6	Questioning	Referring to visual aids
7	Reporting	Concluding your presentation
8	Dealing with questions	Making it interesting
Part 3	**Class seminars**	
	Overview	
	Preparing a presentation	
	Using visual aids, handouts and notes	
	Signposts and language signals	
	Non-verbal communication	
	Asking and dealing with questions	
Part 4	**Strategies for success**	

Acknowledgements

We would like to thank everyone who has contributed to this new edition of *Study Speaking*: the people whose voices are featured on the recording, in order of appearance – Catherine Maclean, Michael Northcott, Susan Warren, Miesbeth Knottenbelt, Miriam Meyerhoff, John MacInnes, Cathy Benson, Pasquale Iannone, Stella Wu and Nuno Vilela; Alan Whyte, who supervised the recording; the teachers and students who piloted the materials and provided helpful feedback; our successive editors at Cambridge University Press, Mickey Bonin and Will Capel; and Hart McLeod for design and layout.

PART 1

Scenarios

Scenario 1 Language centre

Role A Student

It is the week before the start of the academic year. Earlier this week you took the English matriculation test for international students, and scored as follows.

Listening	61%
Reading	68%
Writing	63%
Average	**64%**

According to the results letter from the Language Centre, your average score is slightly above IELTS 6.5 and you are not required to take any additional English classes. When you took IELTS for your application to the university, you scored 6.0, which was the minimum acceptable score.

However, since arriving at the university, you have realised that most of the other students on your degree course are native speakers of English, and you feel you will be at a disadvantage because of your language level. Your scores seem rather low to you; you are used to getting 80% or more on the English courses in your home country.

The Language Centre runs first-term evening courses in listening, reading and writing. You applied to take all three, but you have had a letter from the course director saying the courses were only open to people with lower scores than you. You have made an appointment to speak to the course director, to see if he will allow you onto the courses. What reasons can you give him for needing to take further tuition?

Scenario 2 Library

It is the last week of the vacation before the start of the academic year, when your academic course begins. Last week you completed a pre-sessional language course and this week you want to spend working on the preliminary reading list of books that you have been sent for your degree course. According to the instructions from your department, students are expected to have read the main items on the list before term (semester) starts.

Although some of the books are available in the bookshops, they are very expensive. You have been told that there are copies of all of them in the departmental library. The problem is that this week the library is only open in the afternoon, and one of the other students has told you that the librarian has decided not to lend books this week.

You have decided to go to the library and see whether the librarian will allow you to borrow books. Can you think of good reasons that might persuade her to lend you the books you need? Can you think of alternatives for if she refuses to let you have all the books?

Scenario 3 Finding accommodation

Role A : Student

The university term (semester) has already started and you still don't have permanent accommodation. You are staying in a guest house, which you are finding very expensive. You need to find accommodation urgently because your family is coming to join you in a month's time.

What you want is a flat (apartment) with the following features:

- two bedrooms and plenty of space
- a maximum rent of [_____] per month
- near your university department, to save you travel time and money.

There are two ways of finding a flat. One way is to go through the University Accommodation Service; the other is to look for a private flat, but that tends to be more expensive.

You have already been twice to the Accommodation Service. The same man dealt with you both times. He offered two different flats, but neither of them was suitable. You feel that the man is beginning to lose patience with you. However, you have made another appointment to see him because one of the students doing your course has told you there are some unoccupied university flats near your department. You don't know why the Accommodation Officer has not mentioned them to you.

Plan what to say at your new appointment, to find out more about these unoccupied flats. Think of ways of persuading the Accommodation Officer to let you see one of them.

Scenario 4 Deadline for an essay

Role A : Student

Today is Thursday. You have two weeks to go before the end of your first term (semester). You're working on an essay which has to be handed in by 5 p.m. on Friday (tomorrow).

You are normally quite well-organised and you know that you have worked hard on this particular essay, but you have realised that you're not going to be able to finish it in time for tomorrow's deadline.

The main problem has been that you have been waiting for one specific book on your home country, to use in the essay. The only copy of the book in the University Library had been borrowed by another student. You asked for the book to be recalled, but it came back to the Library only yesterday. You need time to read and analyse the information in the book, and you think that will take you at least another two days. You reckon you should be able to finish the essay by Sunday.

You want to ask the tutor who set the essay to give you an extension of the deadline until Monday. Unfortunately, she is well-known for being very strict about deadlines. Earlier this term you were ill and the tutor agreed to give you an extension for another essay, but you think it's going to be difficult to persuade her this time.

What is the best way to ask for the deadline to be extended to Monday? What can you say if the tutor is unwilling to let you have an extension?

Scenario 5 Examination results

Role A : Student

It is the beginning of the second term (semester) of your university course. At the end of last term your class did a 'mock' exam and you didn't do very well. In fact you hadn't really expected to do well, because most of the course topics were new to you. But the topics for the second term are more familiar so you expect to do better on them.

You feel determined to work harder this term, too. That may mean you have to concentrate on your studies and avoid the various distractions, such as the sports and social activities that took up some of your time in Term 1.

The Director of Studies for the course has asked you to come and see him to discuss your exam results. If your marks weren't very good, what reasons can you give to explain them and to show that you expect to do better now?

Scenario 6 Changing accommodation

Role A : Student

You are staying in a hall of residence (dormitory) run by your university. There are two problems with your room. The first is that the building is quite old – from the 1960s – and so your room is cold, even when the heating is on. You can't really study there comfortably and you have to use the university library, which is 20 minutes' walk away.

The second problem is that the students who live in the rooms around yours are a lot younger than you and make a lot of noise at night, so you can't concentrate when you need to work in your room.

You've tried complaining to the Accommodation Manager about the cold and the noise. She suggested you should put on another layer of clothes when you feel cold and ask the students to be quieter when their noise disturbs you.

University accommodation is relatively expensive in the city and you have had to pay for your room in advance. You think the university may operate this system of payment in advance to discourage students from moving. The rental contract you signed was for a minimum of six months and you had to sign it before seeing the rooms, which you feel was unfair.

Because of these problems, you've decided to speak to the Accommodation Manager to see if you can move to a different hall of residence, where the students are a bit older and quieter and where the rooms are warmer. What can you tell her to persuade her to let you change accommodation?

Scenario 7 Project results

You handed in a project for your course a couple of weeks ago. It was on a topic that you are interested in and you felt it would get quite a good mark.

The results were given out yesterday and your mark was much lower than you expected – a low Pass (54%). In their written comments, the two markers criticised your Introduction as 'rambling' and 'messy'. You are not quite sure what that means. Some of their other comments did not seem fair. In fact, before you gave in the project, you had shown a draft to one of the tutors, who said it was 'OK'.

You have also seen some of the projects written by other students and their work didn't seem better than yours, but they got higher marks. You have asked to speak to the Course Director to ask him to read the project and give a third opinion, to see whether he thinks the mark is fair.

What do you think is the best way to explain to him why you want him to read your project? Discuss what to say.

Scenario 8 Research proposal

Role A Student

You are at the end of the first year as a research student. You are hoping to register to do a PhD. The university operates a 'probationary year' system, in which students who want to do a PhD spend one year as a 'supervised postgraduate student', doing the preliminary work for their thesis. At the end of the year they present a Research Proposal to a committee of three people from their Department – the principal supervisor, the second supervisor and a third person.

You met your research committee last week to present your Proposal, but the meeting did not go well. All three committee members were very critical of your work. They decided that the Proposal was not good enough and they gave you six months to improve it and resubmit it to them. You think this is unfair, so you sent an email to the Head of Department, complaining about the committee's decision.

You have encountered various problems over the past year. The first one is that you're not really very interested in the research topic you are working on. You didn't choose the topic yourself; it was specified by your government, who are paying your fees. The second problem is that your main supervisor is extremely busy and is often away at conferences. In fact you have had relatively little contact with him; you have only managed to meet him six or seven times during the year. This is the main reason for your complaint. The committee also said your written English was poor, but your supervisor hadn't said anything about that before.

The Head of Department has now asked you to come and see her. You hope that the committee's decision can be changed. A major practical problem is that your government scholarship is for three years only. If you have to spend six months re-writing your Proposal, that might mean you won't finish your PhD thesis in time. Think of the best way to approach the meeting with the Head of Department.

Scenario 1 Language centre

Role B : Language course director

You are responsible for the English courses provided to help international students taking degree courses at your university. All international students have to take an English language test (with sections on Listening, Reading and Writing) at the start of the academic year. If they score below 60% overall, or if they have a section score of less than 60%, they are required to take the relevant evening courses, which start in week 3 of the first term. Those courses focus on the skills of listening, reading, and writing.

There are always more students than places, so you limit entry into the classes by giving higher priority to the students who have less than satisfactory scores on the matriculation test. In your experience, many of the students who apply to do the courses do not really need further tuition. As a general rule, you do not accept anyone onto the courses who has scored more than 60% on the relevant section of the test. Your policy is to put higher-scoring students on a waiting list for each class. If there are still spare places when the classes start in week 3, you give those places to the students on the waiting list, strictly in order of score (someone with a score of 61% gets higher priority than someone with 67%).

You can make exceptions. For example, if you get a report from a student's department that they are having problems with English, you sometimes accept them with a score of over 60%.

A student has made an appointment to see you. She applied for all three courses, but has scored too high to be accepted automatically. She probably wants you to change your mind, but this year there is greater demand for courses than ever before. How will you deal with her request? What alternative can you offer her?

Scenario 2 Library

Role B Librarian

You are the head librarian of a departmental library. It is Monday afternoon of the last week of the summer vacation and you are preparing for the beginning of the academic year next week by doing your annual stocktaking. Normally, you would have the help of the assistant librarian but she is away on holiday. So you are doing the stocktaking on your own. Because of this you have decided to keep the library closed in the mornings this week, so as to allow you to work uninterrupted. So for this week only, the opening hours are 2–5 p.m., Monday to Friday.

There are very few students around at the moment, so you have decided not to lend books this week. Any students that come in asking to borrow items from the library can be told to wait until term starts. Alternatively, they can use the main university library, which is open at its normal times – 9 a.m. to 5 p.m. on weekdays.

A foreign student comes in and asks about borrowing books from the library. How can you make it clear to him that you are not allowing any borrowing this week? Is there some alternative you can offer?

Scenario 3 Finding accommodation

Role B Accommodation officer

You work in the Accommodation Service office of the University. It's the first week of the term (semester) and you are extremely busy. An international student came to see you a couple of weeks ago looking for a two-bedroom flat (apartment). You offered her a flat that you thought was exactly what she wanted, but she didn't like it. You offered her another one, and she didn't like that one, either. She seems to be quite difficult to please.

The student has made another appointment to see you today. Usually, the Accommodation Service tries to give priority to international students, because they are often unable to arrange accommodation in advance. Now that the term has started, it is getting really difficult to find flats of the type the student wants.

There is in fact a block of two-bedroom university flats very close to the student's department, but at the moment the flats are being modernised and redecorated. The work will probably not be finished for three or four weeks, so you didn't mention them to the student when she came in before. When the flats are ready, the rent will be [   ] per month, excluding service charges (heating, lighting and telephone).

You have one large two-bedroom flat which you think will suit the student. It's about 10 minutes by bus from her department. The rent is [   ] a month, including all charges (except the telephone). You have decided that if she doesn't accept this flat, you are going to recommend her to look for private accommodation.

Discuss how you can give her that advice without appearing to be unhelpful. After all, it's your job to find students the accommodation they need.

Scenario 4 Deadline for an essay

Role B Tutor

The students on one of the courses you teach are working on an essay that you set them for tomorrow (Friday). The deadline by which they have to hand in their essays is 5 p.m.

One of the students has asked to see you and is probably going to ask for an extension of the deadline. Your department has no fixed policy about what to do when students miss deadlines. Your own rule is that if an essay comes in late without a good reason you take 10% off the final mark.

This particular student has already had one extension on an earlier essay, when he was ill. But he doesn't seem to be a very good student; he misses some lectures and comes in late to others.

This week you have a lot of work. Next week you are running a one-day conference for specialists in your field, so you plan to do all the marking (grading) of the students' essays this weekend. That will make it very difficult for you to accept a late essay unless there are exceptional reasons for doing so.

What will you say to the student if he asks you to extend his deadline? In what circumstances will you agree? What reasons will you give for not extending the deadline?

Scenario 5 Examination results

Role B: Director of Studies

It's the first week of the second term (semester) of the university year. The students you are responsible for took a 'mock' exam at the end of last term. You have arranged a meeting with each student to give them their results.

One of the international students on the course is causing you and the other lecturers special concern. The questions she asks in your lectures suggest that she misunderstands quite basic points. It is not clear whether this is due to her poor English or to her lack of background knowledge. She contributes very little to tutorial discussions and her only piece of written work – apart from the mock exam paper – was very disorganised and hard to follow.

In the mock exam most of this student's answers were off the point; her overall result was a Fail. You and your colleagues have discussed her case at a course meeting and the general view is that she is at risk of failing the course. In the light of her apparent language problems, it was decided at the meeting that she should be required to attend an evening English course this term.

The student is on her way to your room to get her exam result. You need to think carefully how best to make clear to her the seriousness of her situation, because her listening is relatively weak.

Scenario 6 Changing accommodation

Role B Accommodation manager

It's halfway through the first term (semester) of the university year. One of the international students staying in the hall of residence (dormitory) that you manage has made an appointment to see you. He is a mature student, in his forties, and seems to be finding it hard to study again. He has complained in the last month that his room is cold and noisy. He tends to wear quite thin clothes and you advised him to get some jumpers to help him feel warmer. You can't really do much about the noise, which comes from the younger students living in rooms nearby.

You think this student may want to move to another room or possibly to a different university residence. At the moment you have no other rooms available. It's possible that a room may be vacated at the end of the term, because one or two students move out. For example, there is one PhD student who should be going home then, if she passes her oral exam.

Think about how best to deal with the student's complaints. Plan what strategy to use if he asks you to allow him to move.

Scenario 7 Project results

Role B : Course Director

One of the international students in your Department has made an appointment to see you, to discuss a recent project mark. She got a low Pass.

The two colleagues who marked her project thought that her project was very repetitive. One of them, in particular, felt that the introduction to the project was 'rambling' (vague and unfocused) and the other described it as 'messy' (poorly organised). Both the markers had the impression that the student did not know enough about the subject. They also commented on the low standard of her written English, which is much weaker than her ability to communicate in speech.

In your Department, the normal procedure is that if the two markers give similar marks, and agree on a final mark, there is no reason for a third opinion. If they differ by 10% or more and can't agree on a final mark, they ask you as Course Director to assess the student's work and see which of the two marks you agree with more.

In this case, the two markers' individual marks were 50% and 61%. They discussed their comments and then agreed on a mark of 54%. So if the student wishes to make a formal objection to the project mark, you can either read the project yourself and give a third opinion, or you can ask the External Examiner to read the project and to advise you on a suitable mark. That is done near the end of the academic year, just before the Examination Board meeting to discuss students' marks for all their assignments and exams.

Plan how best to explain the situation to the student. You want to be sympathetic but you are also extremely busy at this time of year.

Scenario 8 Research proposal

Role B : Head of Department

The university where you work operates a 'probationary year' system for PhD students. This means that students who want to do a PhD have to spend their first year as a 'supervised postgraduate student', doing the preliminary work for their research and seeing their supervisor for at least six meetings. At the end of the year they present a Research Proposal to a committee of three academics in the Department – the principal supervisor, the second supervisor and a third person.

One of the international students in your Department has emailed you complaining of unfair treatment. His research committee rejected his Research Proposal, for two reasons. Firstly, they felt it didn't have an adequate theoretical basis. Secondly, they were worried about the student's level of written English, which is much weaker than his spoken English. The student has not explained in what way he thinks he has been unfairly treated.

You agree with the committee's decision, which was to ask the student to improve his Proposal and to resubmit it in six months' time. You also think he should take classes in academic writing, which the university provides free of charge. If the revised version is acceptable, the student can then register as a PhD student.

You have asked the student to come and see you, because you want to hear his side of the story. Think about the questions you want to ask him. Also, plan how to tell the student that you agree with the decision of your three colleagues on the research committee.

PART 2

Discussion skills and

Presentation skills

UNIT 1 Work

This unit aims to develop your speaking skills by:

1 increasing your confidence in expressing opinions in discussions

2 improving your ability to structure presentations effectively.

DISCUSSION SKILLS
Giving your opinion

The main purpose of academic discussion – for example, tutorials and seminars – in the Western educational tradition is for individuals to exchange opinions on the topics being studied. This is true at both undergraduate and postgraduate levels of study. You are expected to express and justify your own views, not simply to repeat information you have been told in books and lectures. The focus of this Unit is expressing opinions about controversial topics. Unit 2 will deal with expressing agreement or disagreement with other people in the discussion.

Useful language

more formal	It is my view that...
	I take the view that...
	I believe...
neutral	I think...
	What I think is...
	I'd say that...
	It seems to me that...
	It seems clear/obvious/evident to me that...
	I have to say that...
	I'm (not) persuaded that...
less formal	As far as I'm concerned,...
	To me,...

You may be surprised to learn that one expression which is <u>not</u> very common in spoken discussion is *In my opinion*…! Non-native speakers of English seem to use this expression much more than native speakers do.

Practice

In small groups, practise using these expressions by *quickly* giving your opinion about:

- smoking
- public transport
- cloning animals
- the Internet
- the state of the economy
- crime in your country
- spiders
- politicians
- traffic in your cities.

Discussion point 1: What work means to you
Preparation (individual)

Which of these factors would be most important to you in choosing a job? Decide on your top three priorities, and rank them in order (1 = most important, 2 = second most important, 3 = third most important).

- high salary ✓
- job security ✓
- interesting work
- pleasant working environment
- good relationships with colleagues and superiors
- opportunities for promotion and career development
- enough holidays and free time
- short journey to work

How would you complete this sentence?

'For me, work is…
 …the way to achieve the lifestyle I want.'
 …the way to ensure financial security for myself and my family.'
 …my main interest or purpose in life.'
 …the fulfilment of my years of study and training.'
 …just something everyone has to do.'
 …how I can achieve status in society.'
 …how I gain recognition and respect in my professional field.'
 …how I can do my duty to my country.'
 …something else.' Give details.

Discussion

1 Form a group with other students. Compare your answers to the above questions.
2 Do you think your parents would have given similar answers to you? And your grandparents? Give reasons for your answer.
3 Do you think workers in your country suffer discrimination because of either gender or age?

Discussion point 2
Preparation 1 (individual)

Read this excerpt from a BBC radio programme about changes in working practices in Britain. After the presenter's introduction, two retired men describe what working life in manufacturing industry was like when they were young. (Some vocabulary is explained on page 38.)

John Fortune (presenter)

Travelling on the train down to Bristol, the man opposite me gets out his mobile and rings his secretary to say, "We're just passing Reading. Can you ring me if there're any emails?" This is the new way of working – clean, high-tech, industrious – with none of those shoddy practices of the past. Does it really matter no-one's too sure what we actually *do*? We're an 'enterprise culture', a 'knowledge economy', and our fastest-growing job-market is in – call centres, which employ more than all the men and women in mining, steel and car-production combined. But *something* had to change…
(Noise of machinery)

Dave Bannon (retired worker)

Back in the early sixties, there must have been close to, nearly 2,500 people on this site. Not the site we're currently on now, but across the way, in the old smelter. Blimey, the site was huge!

John Goddard (retired worker)

You just wondered where all these people worked! It was almost like they came in, got paid, and went home again.

John Fortune

Down at the head of the River Avon, there's a huge zinc smelter, where Dave Bannon and John Goddard both started work. Or is 'work' the word I mean?

John Goddard

You could certainly get away with having a kip in the afternoon. There were several guys who I can remember used to regularly nod off in the afternoon, and this guy, I remember, used to smoke Capstan Full Strength cigarettes, and his ledgers was always covered in burn marks where he'd dropped his cigarette, or lines across it, what we called 'zizzers' back in those days, where he'd nodded off, and the pencil or the pen had gone straight across the ledgers there. But people just accepted it.

Transcribed from *British manufacturing: my part in its downfall.*
BBC Radio 4. Sunday, 17 November 2002.

call centre	a place where many people are employed to deal with customers by telephone
blimey!	(British colloquial) expression of astonishment
smelter	a factory where metal is separated from the rock that contains it (ore)
shoddy	of a low standard
kip	(British colloquial) nap, short sleep during the day
guy	(colloquial) man
ledger	a book for keeping the financial records of a company
nod off	fall asleep

Preparation 2 (individual)

You are going to discuss the following question.

What have been the most significant changes in working life in the last 10–20 years?

Think about the situation in *your* country. It may be helpful to consider the aspects of work listed here:

- the type of work available
- employment rates
- working hours
- attitudes to work
- pay and conditions
- participation of women
- working age
- effect of technology.

You may think of other aspects. Have these changes been for the better?

Discussion

1 Now work in a group with other students. Compare your ideas on the question above. Do you think the situation in your own country is typical of the world in general, or a part of it?

2 What changes in working life do you expect to see in the next 10–20 years?

3 The recorded talk in the *Presentation skills* section of this Unit is on the topic of work and family. Is it possible for a woman to be a successful mother and have a successful professional career? Should society encourage or discourage women from combining the two?

PRESENTATION SKILLS
Structuring your presentation
Being clear about your objective

Being clear about your objective is the first and most important rule for giving an effective presentation. If you yourself are not clear about the main message of your presentation, then your audience will find your presentation confusing.

When you are deciding on your objective, you have to take into account both what *you know* about the topic and what *your audience knows*. You also need to take into account the *context* and *purpose* of the presentation. Here are some examples.

- If you have been asked to present a topic to a seminar group, you will provide a basic overview, with suggestions for further reading.
- If you are presenting your own research at a conference, you will explain the background to your research question, outline your method, state your main results, and then offer a brief comment on the results before inviting questions.
- If you are presenting your research to members of your own department, you may not need to explain the background to the research question, but on the other hand you may wish to demonstrate to your tutor that you have read the relevant literature; and you may wish to take the opportunity to have members of the group discuss questions you have about the research method or interpretation of results.

So it is important to be clear about the objective of your presentation, so that you can focus the content appropriately for the context.

Organising the information

Academic presentations are not like after-dinner speeches. Their main function is not to entertain but to provide information. So it is vitally important that the information is presented clearly. Ways of organising the information include:

- chronological sequence
- most important to least important
- general to particular
- one point of view compared with another point of view.

Using familiar information structures like these helps the audience to follow your presentation more easily.

Signalling the structure

Planning a well-structured presentation is not enough. When you actually give your presentation, you must make its structure clear to the listeners. Remember: you may have a plan and know the structure of your talk, but the listeners do not know it unless you tell them! They need to be guided through the spoken information. To do this, you need to use what are often called *signposts* and *language signals.*

'Signposting' gives an advance view of the organisation of the whole presentation, or of the next section.

Examples of 'signposting'

1 Organisation of the whole presentation

   First *I will tell you something about the historical background,* ***then*** *I will present the two main theories which are currently under discussion,* ***and finally*** *I will add some personal comments deriving from our recent research.*

2 Organisation of the next section

   There are ***three reasons*** *why we do this: these are* ***economic****,* ***legal****, and* ***psychological****. The* ***economic*** *argument is...*

Language signals are words and phrases that tell the listener where you are in the presentation, where you are taking them next and where they have just been. They may signal either: the topic of the whole talk; the beginning or end of a section of the talk; a new point in a list; a contrasting point; an example; or a point of special importance.

Examples of language signals

1 The topic of the talk

   I want to focus on

2 A complete section

   And now I'd like to turn to the issue of long working hours

3 A new point in a list

   Secondly, unemployment causes social unrest

4 A contrasting point

   However, others believe that a woman's place is in the home

---

5 An example

In some countries, for example India and Thailand, child labour is a fact of economic life

6 A point of special importance

...and here I would like to emphasise the importance of training

The distinction between signposting and language signals is not important. Indeed, some people use the terms interchangeably. But taken together their function is important. If the main points of your talk are well-organised AND clearly signalled, you are well on the way to making an effective and clear presentation.

For more examples of the signposts and language signals that are frequently used in academic presentations, see Checklist 3 on page 122.

Analysis

The listening extract on the cassette comes from one of a series of presentations and workshops on the subject of work. The talk is organised as follows.

1 The speaker signals the topic for this talk, 'work-family balance', and gives definitions and examples.
2 She speaks more particularly about one aspect of research on work-family balance – how to gather the views of children – and gives an example from her own research.
3 She signposts the route ahead, saying what she plans to do for the rest of the seminar session.

FIRST LISTENING

As you listen, indicate to your teacher when you hear the start of each section.

SECOND LISTENING

As you listen, write down the words and phrases used by the speaker:
- to signpost
- to signal examples.

Check your notes with your partner. Then the teacher will collect the phrases and write them on the board. You might like to listen a third time to hear the phrases again in context.

Presentation practice

STAGE 1: PREPARATION

Plan a short talk (two to three minutes) on the topic of work.
EITHER choose one aspect from the following:

- working hours
- equal pay for men and women
- sick leave
- holidays
- work and child care
- work and family time
- child labour
- job security
- interesting or boring?
- unemployment
- manual work and office work
- work and personal fulfilment
- self-employment
- retirement from work

OR you may plan your talk on any other aspect of work that you
prefer.

Plan what you will say about the aspect of work that you have
chosen. Make *very* short notes – just a word or two – under each of
the following headings:

- Introduction (state your choice of topic)
- Main point 1 (plus example)
- Main point 2 (plus example)
- Conclusion

The Conclusion can be signalled with *So*, or *Finally*, or *To conclude*.
    For the other sections of your talk, choose from the examples of
signposts and signals in the boxes on pages 40 and 41, or in your
notes from the listening activity.

STAGE 2: PRACTICE

1 Practise your talk by speaking to one other student. They should
   take notes of your main points.
2 When you have finished your talk, look at their notes.
   - Have they understood all your main points?
   - Have they recognised your language signals?
3 Discuss what you should do to make your meaning clearer.
   - Should you change the structure (plan) of the talk?
   - Should you change the details of the talk?
   - Should you signal your main points more clearly?
4 Then exchange roles with your partner.

STAGE 3: PRESENTATION

Now work with two other students (not with the same partner as in Stage 2) and take turns in giving your talk a second time. Pay particular attention to the way you signal a move to a new section. Check afterwards whether the listeners' notes match what you intended to say. Is any essential information missing from their notes?

STAGE 4: EVALUATION

What did you find when you looked at the other students' notes? Which of the following did you discover?

a) They both understood all your main points.

b) They differed in what they had understood.

c) They had misunderstood one or more parts.

SUMMARY

Important steps in achieving an effective presentation are:

1 Specify the objective to yourself, precisely.
2 Select the content.
3 Organise the content in a clear and logical order.
4 Use signposts and language signals to present the organised content clearly to your listeners.

UNIT 2 Food

This unit aims to develop your speaking skills by:
1. improving your confidence in expressing agreement and disagreement in discussions
2. helping you use an appropriate speaking style in presentations.

DISCUSSION SKILLS
Agreeing and disagreeing

To participate properly in tutorials and seminars you will be expected to give your own opinions, as we practised doing in Unit 1, and also to respond to other people's ideas. You will need to express both agreement and disagreement.

Agreeing is easier than disagreeing in discussions. If you agree with what someone has said, it is often enough just to say 'yes', or even simply nod. If you want to disagree, you will be expected to explain why you think the speaker is wrong. You may also be worried that you will cause unintended offence if you choose the wrong words to express your disagreement.

Fortunately, you don't have to use especially polite language to disagree. If you listen to how native English speakers signal disagreement, even in academic discussions, you will find that the most common way of doing this is simply to begin 'But...'.

Useful language

Agreeing	*Yes.*
	Yes, that's right.
	Yes, that's true.
	Yes, you're (quite/absolutely) right.
	Yes, I agree.
	That's a good point.
	That's what I think.
	Absolutely.
Partly agreeing	*Yes, OK, but...*
	I see what you mean, but...
	I take your point, but...
	I accept that, but...
	That may be true, but...

Expressing doubt/weak disagreement	*I'm not sure about that.*
	Is there any evidence for that?
Disagreeing	*But...*
	But surely...
	But don't you think...?
	But you can't really mean...?
	But there's no evidence for that.
	But that goes against...
	But what about...?
	I don't (really) agree (with you/that...).
	I don't think that's right/true.
	I don't see how you can say...

Practice

Work in pairs or small groups. Look at each question in turn. One student should give a brief answer to the question, and the other(s) should then agree or disagree. Choose appropriate expressions from the list above. Try to use a different expression each time you agree or disagree.

1 Many countries require their male (and sometimes female) citizens to do a period of compulsory military service. Do you approve of this idea?
2 Do you think the streets in this town or city are kept clean enough?
3 One solution to the problem of overpopulation may be to colonise other planets. Do you think this is a serious possibility?
4 Should mothers of young children go to work?
5 Some people believe the best way to improve your English is to study grammar books. Do you agree?
6 'When in Rome do as the Romans do.' Is this your own attitude to living in a different country?

Discussion point 1: Your food choices
Preparation (individual)

When you choose food in a shop or supermarket, which of the following aspects do you take into account?

a) country of origin
b) price
c) ease of preparation
d) your (or your family's) health
e) taste
f) how it was produced
g) other factors (what?)

Rank the factors (above) from 1 to 7 according to your *personal* priorities (1 = most important; 7 = least important).

Discussion

Now form a small group with other students. Compare and discuss your priorities.

- How closely do your priorities agree with the others'? If your opinions differ, explain why.
- Do you think your priorities are typical of people from your country?

Discussion point 2: GM food

Preparation 1 (groups)

1 In groups, discuss what you understand by the following terms. If you are not sure, use a dictionary or ask your teacher.
   a) nutrient/nutritious
   b) genetically modified (GM) or 'biotech' crops
   c) grain
   d) seed
   e) harvest
   f) yield
   g) fertilisers
   h) pesticides
   i) herbicides
   j) insecticides

2 Briefly discuss the following question.

Has the use of GM crops received much attention in your country – for example, in the media or amongst people in general?

Preparation 2 (individual)

Your tutor will ask you to read one or two short texts summarising research on the use of GM, or 'biotech', crops for food production. When you have read the texts and understood them (use a dictionary, or ask your tutor for help, if necessary), prepare to report the content of your text(s) to the other members of your group.

Discussion

1 Take it in turns to explain the main ideas in your text. When you listen to the others, *make notes* on the main arguments *for* and *against* GM crops. Ask for clarification if there is anything you didn't understand.
2 Now discuss the following question in your group.

Should the use of GM food crops be encouraged?

Make a conscious effort to vary the way you express agreement and disagreement. Try to extend your range of expression by using expressions from pages 44 and 45 which you have not used before.

TEXT 1 [Source: US Department of State; discussion paper]

A MORE PRODUCTIVE AGRICULTURAL SECTOR

It is important to understand that biotechnology has enormous potential benefits. Not least among these benefits is the potential to reduce the environmental impact of agriculture.

Some biotech crops can decrease the need for pesticides and herbicides to control pests, weeds, and plant diseases and allow more selective application of agricultural chemicals.

Scientists are also looking at ways to use biotech to deliver more nutrients and better taste in our foods. Damaging deficiencies in Vitamin A and other nutrients among the poor worldwide may well be addressed cost-effectively through biotech agriculture. Another potential benefit of biotech is increased income for farmers, both small and large. For example, biotechnology has improved the quality of seed grains and the ability to produce bigger harvests from currently cultivated land. Equally important, increased yields and reduced chemical and labor costs can represent increased income for the farmer. Finally, farmers can save in the cost of bringing their product to market with biotech crops that are easier to store, need no refrigeration, and have a longer shelf-life.

(Abriged from) Larsen, Alan. "Biotechnology: Finding a practical approach to a promising technology." *Economic Perspectives*, October 1999. http://usinfo.state.gov/journals/ites/1099/ijee/bio-larson.htm (8 January 2004).

TEXT 2 [Source: The Soil Association (organisation promoting organic farming); summary of research survey]

Genetically engineered food: still unlabelled and untested, Greenpeace, 2001

This survey of the scientific literature on GMOs found that at this time there had been only three published studies of the health effects of consuming GMOs, and none of these animal feeding trials were longer than 70 days. Other published studies that have been used as evidence of safety by the Government and biotechnology companies were in fact only tests of the health effects of the modified protein, not the whole GMO, i.e. most existing 'safety' studies have not tested the side effects of the engineering process which is the main health concern.

The Soil Association. "Evidence of the benefits of organic farming." 26 July 2002 http://www.soilassociation.org/sa/saweb.nsf/librarytites/Briefing_Sheets05092001 (8 January 2004).

TEXT 3 [Source: Monsanto (biotechnology company); media briefing]

Q: How are foods produced using biotechnology established as safe and adequately regulated?

A: Years of research and testing have shown that commercially available foods developed through agricultural biotechnology are substantially equivalent to foods developed through traditional plant breeding and are safe to eat. The term "substantially equivalent" is used by scientists and regulatory agencies to indicate that the composition of these foods is basically the same as conventional foods and that the nutritional content is the same.

Among others, the Nuffield Council on Bioethics, Organization for Economic Cooperation and Development (OECD), Food and Agriculture Organization of the United Nations (FAO), World Health Organization (WHO), International Life Sciences Institute (ILSI) and the National Academy of Sciences of seven nations have all confirmed the safety of biotech products.

Monsanto Company. "Media briefing FAQs."
http://www.monsanto.com/monsanto/media/press_kit/faqs/default.htm (11 May 2002).

TEXT 4 [Source: Monsanto (biotechnology company); media briefing]

Q: Despite claims otherwise, isn't it true that agricultural biotechnology cannot relieve world hunger?

A: No one with any real knowledge of the subject would claim that agricultural biotechnology alone can relieve world hunger. However, without the contributions of agricultural biotechnology, it will be difficult, if not impossible, to relieve world hunger.

Such organizations as the Nuffield Council on Bioethics, World Bank, World Health Organization (WHO) and Food and Agriculture Organization of the United Nations (FAO) have indicated that agricultural biotechnology will help alleviate world hunger by increasing food production. Biotechnology can increase the quantity of the harvest by addressing the factors that traditionally deplete crops: pests, weeds and disease. Furthermore, biotech crops will grow in inhospitable climates making it possible to farm in areas that have previously been uncultivated.

Monsanto Company. "Media briefing FAQs."
http://www.monsanto.com/monsanto/media/press_kit/faqs/default.htm (11 May 2002).

TEXT 5 [Source: The Soil Association (organisation promoting organic farming); summary of UN report]

Agriculture: Towards 2015/30, Technical Report, FAO, April 2000

This United Nations report shows that GM crops are not needed to feed the world's growing population. Several forward projections to 2030 when the world's population is expected to be over 8 billion, found that, leaving aside GM crops, the potential of current agricultural resources and technological knowledge are already sufficient to ensure that total crop production "will exceed population growth".

The Soil Association. "Evidence of the benefits of organic farming." 26 July 2002. http://www.soilassociation.org/sa/saweb.nsf/librarytites/Briefing_Sheets05092001 (8 January 2004).

TEXT 6 [Source: Independent on Sunday (UK newspaper); news report]

GM FOOD WILL NOT EASE HUNGER

BY GEOFFREY LEAN
Environment Editor

Britain's top aid charities have told the Prime Minister that genetically modified foods will not solve world hunger, but may actually increase poverty and malnutrition.

Their intervention – in a joint submission to the Government's official debate on GM crops and foods – strikes a devastating blow at a central plank of its support for the controversial technology.

The charity leaders say claims that GM crops will feed the world are "misleading and fail to address the complexities of poverty reduction". They acknowledge that the technology may have "potential benefits" but are concerned they will not help the small farmers and poor people in the rural Third World where their groups have practical experience.

The charities say GM crops are likely to create more poverty. They point out that hunger is not caused by a shortage of food, but because the poor cannot afford to buy it.

In the past, new agricultural technologies have tended to be taken up by rich farmers. They increase production and force poor farmers out of business.

The charities fear that introducing GM will have even more catastrophic effects because it is dominated by a few multinational companies.

Lean, Geoffrey. "GM food will not ease hunger." *Independent on Sunday*, 10 November 2002: 2.

PRESENTATION SKILLS
Speaking in an appropriate style
Formal and informal styles

The following sentences express similar meanings. Which is most formal in style? Which is least formal? Would all examples be appropriate in an academic presentation?

A Lots of people don't have enough money to get food.
B Many people don't have enough money to buy food.
C Poverty and hunger are widespread.
D Many people do not have sufficient money to purchase food.

Sentence **A** is the least formal. It is conversational in style, with the short verb form and basic vocabulary. It is NOT appropriate for an academic presentation, but it might be acceptable in the discussion that follows a presentation, especially in an informal seminar group.

Sentence **B** is more formal, but is still in a simple speaking style, with the shortened verb form. The vocabulary is simple but precise. It would be appropriate for an academic presentation.

Sentence **C** is more formal than **B**. It is typical of academic speaking and writing, short and clear, with abstract nouns. It, too, would be appropriate for a presentation.

Sentence **D** is also more formal than **B**. The vocabulary is more elaborate, but does not add precision, and for that reason many people would prefer **B**. If the entire presentation were in the style of sentence **D**, it would sound heavy and pompous.

Academic speaking style

A presentation composed entirely of long heavy sentences would be monotonous. Similarly, a presentation composed entirely of short plain sentences would be monotonous. In practice, therefore, most effective speakers mix styles **B**, **C** and **D** – often to good effect. For example, a short plain sentence after longer sentences can sound dramatic and catch attention.

Speakers also vary in their choice of a more or less informal personal style. You will have the opportunity to evaluate different speakers' styles when you listen to the different recorded examples later in each unit. But although there is a degree of choice it is important to keep in mind that:

- an academic presentation is not a casual conversation with a friend, so a very informal speaking style is not appropriate
- an academic presentation is spoken, not written – so reading aloud a typical written academic text is not appropriate.

An appropriate academic speaking style falls between the two extremes, as shown below.

informal	*academic*	*formal*
speaking style	*presentation style*	*academic written style*

Signposts and language signals

Signposts and language signals are another important feature of academic presentation style. (See Unit 1 and Checklist 3 on page 122.)

Analysis

All the sentences below would be acceptable in an academic presentation. You will hear some of them when you listen to the recording. Before listening, decide which sentence in each pair is more formal, and which less formal.

1. a) *We're just beginning to find out that this is a problem.*
   b) *The problem is only now being discovered.*
2. a) *In Mexico they recently discovered that pollen had spread hundreds of miles.*
   b) *Pollen was found to have spread hundreds of miles in Mexico.*
3. a) *The human population is projected to peak at 10 billion in the 21st century.*
   b) *Scientists think that there will be 10 billion humans in the 21st century.*
4. a) *Because there will be more people, we will need more food.*
   b) *The greatly increased population will require increased farm outputs.*

FIRST LISTENING

Now listen to the short talk on genetically modified food. This presentation has an argument structure. Take short notes to answer the following key questions.

1. Why is there concern about genetically modified food?
2. What are the arguments for genetically modified food?
3. What are the counter-arguments?

Then compare your notes with those of another student. Do you agree?

SECOND LISTENING

Listen again to the talk, which the teacher will play in sections.
- Note the signalling phrases used by the speaker.

- The style is appropriate for an academic presentation. It is not like a casual conversation with a friend, nor is it like academic written text. Within these limits, do you think that this speaker's style is rather formal, or rather informal?

Presentation practice

STAGE 1: PREPARATION

Plan a short talk (2–3 minutes) on the topic of the typical diet in your country. The objective of the talk is to give an informative account to listeners who do not know your country and its food. The information might include answers to questions such as: What is the most common food, which people eat every day? Do young people and old people like the same foods? Do most people in your country eat too much, or too little? Is the typical diet healthy?

You cannot include information about all these questions in such a short talk, so you must select and plan.

Decide first what your main message will be. Then organise the content. Look back to page 39 for suggestions on ways of organising the information in a presentation. Make *very* short notes – just a word or two – under each of the following headings:

- Introduction
- Main point 1 (plus example or comment)
- Main point 2 (plus example or comment)
- Conclusion

Before you give your talk, decide which language signals you will use in each section. (See Unit 1 or Checklist 3 on page 122.)

STAGE 2: PRACTICE

1 Practise your talk by speaking to one other student. Although you are speaking to only one person, try to speak in the appropriate academic style, as if you were speaking to your academic tutor or an academic audience. They should take notes of your main points.
2 When you have finished your talk, look at their notes. Have they understood all your main points? If not, discuss what you should do to make your meaning clearer.
3 Ask your partner if they thought your style was appropriate. Was there any part of your talk that was too informal?
4 Then exchange roles with your partner and repeat steps 1–3.

STAGE 3: PRESENTATION

Now work with two other students (not with the same partner as in Stage 2) and take turns in giving your talk a second time. Pay particular attention to using appropriate signals and style.

Check afterwards whether the listeners' notes match what you intended to say. Is any essential information missing from their notes?

STAGE 4: EVALUATION

What did you find when you looked at the other students' notes? Which of the following did you discover?
- They both understood all your main points.
- They differed in what they had understood.
- They had misunderstood one or more parts.

SUMMARY

An academic speaking style should be:
- more formal than in a casual conversation with a friend
- more simple than in academic written style.

An important feature is the use of language signals.

Within these limits, speakers differ from each other in their personal styles.

Within these limits, individual speakers vary their style, often to good effect.

If you listen with awareness of style, you become more confident of recognising what is appropriate and what you are personally comfortable with.

UNIT 3 Language

This unit aims to develop your speaking skills by:

1. increasing your confidence in giving explanations in discussions
2. improving your delivery in presentations.

DISCUSSION SKILLS

Explaining

When you explain something, such as a process, structure, situation or theory, you give the reasons why it is like it is. This involves linking causes (the reasons) with their effects (a description of the thing you are explaining).

In this Unit you will practise explaining some of your beliefs about learning English, and suggesting explanations for your progress, or lack of progress, in one aspect of your English skills.

Useful language

Below are some expressions that are commonly used in spoken explanations of cause and effect.

Identifying causes/reasons

The reason (for…) is (that)…
That's because…
That's because of/due to…
The/One explanation (for…) is (that)…
What has brought this about/led to/caused this…is….
What's responsible for…is….

Can you think of any other expressions to add?

Expressing certainty/uncertainty

The reasons for some things are not certain. When you give explanations, you need to make clear how sure or unsure you are of the reasons you identify. You can begin your explanation with phrases such as the following.

I think   *…that's because/the reason is (etc.)*
It's likely that
I'm certain
I'd say
It could be that

It could well be that
Possibly
I'm sure
There's no doubt (in my mind) (that)

Work with one or two other students and number the above expressions of uncertainty in order of certainty (1 = most certain; 9 = least certain). You may feel that some expressions show the same level of certainty.

Practice

In small groups, practise using the certainty/uncertainty expressions by briefly explaining what you think are the causes *or* effects of some of the following phenomena:

- global warming
- poverty
- crime
- the extinction of the dinosaurs
- drug addiction.

Discussion point 1: Your beliefs about learning English

Preparation (individual)

First, read through this list of statements about learning English[1]. Choose one statement you strongly agree with; one you strongly disagree with; and one you are not sure about.

1 It is easier for children than for adults to learn English as a non-native language.
2 People from my country are good at learning English.
3 It is necessary to know about English-speaking culture in order to speak English successfully.
4 I can learn English better from talking socially to native speakers than by studying.
5 The most important goal in learning English is to increase my vocabulary.
6 Women are better than men at learning English.
7 You can learn English in the same way you learn any other subject.
8 Native English speakers have a different way of thinking from native speakers of my language.
9 I am only learning English because I need it for my studies or job.
10 I feel I have a different personality when I speak English.

[1] Based on Horowitz, Elaine K. "Surveying student beliefs about language learning". *Learner Strategies in Language Learning.* Eds A. Wenden and J. Rubin. Englewood Cliffs: Prentice Hall International, 1987. 127–128.

Discussion

In groups, explain *why* you agree with/disagree with/are unsure about the statements you have chosen. Say whether you agree or not with the opinions expressed by other students.

Discussion point 2: Your experience of learning English

Your group should choose one of the following aspects of English to discuss:

- listening
- speaking
- reading
- writing
- vocabulary.

Preparation (individual)

Think about how your skills in that particular area of English have developed since you started learning English. Have you made more or less progress in that area than in other areas? Why do you think that is? For example, think about:

- the type of teaching you have had
- the strategies you have used by yourself to improve your skills
- the types and amount of practice you have had
- your experience of using your skill in real communication.

Discussion

1 Explain to the others in your group the factors that you believe have contributed to your success, or lack of success, in developing the aspect of your English that you have selected.
2 What do you think are the best strategies or techniques to adopt to improve your skills in this area? (Pay special attention to what people believe has contributed to success!)
3 Write down a list of the suggestions made by your group on ways to improve in the area you have been discussing. Check that all the members of the group have understood all the suggestions.
4 If there is more than one group in your class, your group should report your suggestions to the other group(s). You could choose one student to report all your group's ideas, or take turns. Don't forget to explain the rationale for your suggestions. Be prepared to answer questions.

PRESENTATION SKILLS
Delivery: Emphasis and phrasing
Using your voice
The way you speak when you give a presentation is important. If you say all words with the same emphasis and at the same speed, the presentation will sound boring and it may not be easy to understand. You want listeners to understand your meaning easily, and to be interested in what you are saying.

Using your voice to emphasise important words is one way of doing this. Grouping words into meaningful units, or phrases, also helps to make your presentation more *listener-friendly*. It will be easier to understand your meaning and your presentation will sound less monotonous.

Emphasis
There are several ways in which you can emphasise, or stress, important points with your voice. You can:
- speak the word more loudly
- speak the word more slowly
- be briefly silent before and after the word.

With a partner, try all three techniques in the sentence in the box below. Emphasise the words 'BY FAR'.

English is now BY FAR the most frequently used language in international conferences.

Phrasing
Your presentation will be clearer and more interesting if you group words together according to your meaning.
- Listen to your teacher read Text A with very little phrasing and emphasis, and Text B with more phrasing and emphasis.
- Then with your partner practise saying Text B. Remember to pause very briefly at the end of each line. Emphasise the words in bold print (and only these words).

Text A	Text B
English is now by far the most frequently used language in international conferences. Increasingly, it is the only official language. Simultaneous translation facilities are sometimes provided in very large congresses, but this is becoming less, rather than more, common.	**English** is now **BY FAR** the most **frequently** used language in **international conferences**. **Increasingly** it is the **ONLY official** language. **Simultaneous translation** facilities are **sometimes** provided in very **large** congresses, but this is becoming **LESS**, rather than **MORE**, common.

Analysis

Divide the text below into sensible word groups, or phrases, and underline the words you want to emphasise.

> OK well what I'm going to do is briefly describe the main differences between English and Outlandic you should have in front of you two sets of sentences with the English on top and the Outlandic underneath and what I'm going to do is explain which bit goes with which bit in each language and to try to make clear the main differences between the two languages

- Then compare your version with your partner's. Try saying them aloud to each other, as if you were giving a presentation.
- Are your versions the same? If they are different, do you think one version is better than the other? Why?

FIRST LISTENING

Your teacher will play you the original version of the sentences you have been studying.

Listen to the speaker and mark his phrases and main points of emphasis.

> OK well what I'm going to do is briefly describe the main differences between English and Outlandic you should have in front of you two sets of sentences with the English on top and the Outlandic underneath and what I'm going to do is explain which bit goes with which bit in each language and to try to make clear the main differences between the two languages

Compare what you have just heard with the way you spoke. Was it the same or different? If it was different, which do you prefer and why?

SECOND LISTENING

The text you have been working on was the first part of a seminar presentation about the differences between two languages: English and Outlandic. Your teacher will now play the complete presentation.

- Listen carefully and make notes.
- At the end, ask the teacher for clarification of any points that you have not fully understood.

Presentation practice

IELTS

STAGE 1: PREPARATION

Think about the general differences in grammatical structure between your own language and English. Note down the main points of difference, with an example for each. Among the things you could consider are: tenses, articles, word order, pronouns and question forms.

STAGE 2: PRACTICE

Using your notes, describe the differences to your partner. Remember to group words in complete phrases. Use your voice to emphasise important points. Allow your partner to ask you for any additional clarification they feel they need.

After 5 minutes, exchange the roles of speaker and listener and repeat.

STAGE 3: PRESENTATION

Form a new trio with two other students. Take turns at giving your talk, as the others take notes. Remember to group words into phrases, with stress on the most important words only. Think in particular about ways of making clearer the points that your Stage 2 partner asked you to clarify.

STAGE 4: EVALUATION

Were you able to express yourself more clearly the second time? Did you find it easier in your second talk to group words into phrases and emphasise your meaning?

Did you find it easier to understand your partners when they spoke in this way?

Are there still points that you would like the teacher to help you to put into English?

SUMMARY

The content of a presentation may be clear to *you* as a speaker, but your listeners need to be guided through the spoken information. You can make your meaning clearer by:

- grouping words into phrases
- giving special emphasis to the words that are most important.

Using these techniques will also make your presentation sound less monotonous.

UNIT 4 Health

This unit aims to develop your speaking skills by:

1 improving your confidence in making suggestions in discussions

2 helping you use visual aids effectively in presentations.

DISCUSSION SKILLS

Making suggestions

Academic discussions often involve proposing ways to solve problems. In this Unit we focus on the language you use to make suggestions and recommendations.

Useful language

Making a suggestion means giving your opinion about what should be done, so you often use the same expressions that you use for expressing opinions – see the *Useful language* section in Unit 1.

When you make a suggestion, you can indicate how strong your opinion is. You may find it useful to think of three 'levels' of advice:

suggestion (lowest level – just an idea to be considered)

advice (middle level – what you think should be done)

necessity (highest level – what you *know* must be done).

The following common expressions are often combined with other verbs to indicate the level of advice you are giving. Working with one or two other students, decide which level each one represents – 'suggestion', 'advice' or 'necessity'.

need to   *should*
ought to   *could*
have to   *must*

How would you use *had better*, as in 'You'd better ask the librarian'? Which level of advice would you say it is? How formal is it?

Here are some of the expressions people often use to give suggestions and advice. Again, decide which of the three levels each of the expressions indicates.

formal

I propose (that)...
I would suggest (that)...
My advice would be to...
I think the most effective strategy/course/procedure would be to...
I believe it would be advisable to...
I think it's essential/vital/crucial/urgent/most important that...
Should we consider...-ing?
One option would be to...

neutral

I think what we/you/they should do is...
What I think we/you should do is...
I think it would be a good/sensible idea to...
I think the best way forward would be to...
My feeling is we/you should...
I wonder if you/we should...?
What do you think about the idea of...-ing?
Would there be any advantage/benefit in...-ing?

informal

If you ask me, we/you should...
What about/How about...-ing?
Do you think there would be any mileage in...-ing?
The main/key/most important thing is to...
It might be an idea to...
We/You've really got to...

Practice

In small groups, practise using these expressions by quickly giving your advice on the following problems. Each person in the group should try to suggest a different solution. Choose expressions you have not often used before, and try not to repeat an expression that someone else in your group has already used.

a) A friend has gone to study for a year far away from family and friends, and is feeling homesick.

b) Air pollution in your capital city is becoming a serious health risk.

c) Some students at your university or college are having financial difficulties.

d) The crime rate amongst teenagers is rising.

e) A student you know is having difficulty keeping up with the course work.

f) A friend wants to improve his/her English pronunciation.

Discussion Point 1: Health risks

Preparation 1 (individual)

Read this introduction to an article about a World Health Organization report:

WHO sets out world's deadly top 10

Andy Coghlan

Just 10 avoidable risk factors, including malnutrition, unsafe sex, smoking and poor sanitation, account for a massive 40 per cent of global deaths each year, warns the World Health Organization.

The WHO's new data on patterns of death and illness appear in its World Health Report 2002, launched on Wednesday. The WHO says that cheap remedies exist and that governments of all countries can do more to prevent unnecessary and premature death. It concludes that such countermeasures could extend average life expectancy by five to 10 years.

"This report provides a road map for how societies can tackle a wide range of preventable conditions that are killing millions of people prematurely and robbing tens of millions of healthy life," says Gro Harlem Brundtland, WHO director general.

The risks are starkly different between "haves" and "have-nots".

('Haves' and 'have-nots' refer to the rich and the poor.)

What would you guess the ten risk factors to be?

Make a list of *five* factors which you think most endanger people's health in poorer countries, and another list of *five* for richer countries. The items in your lists should be the potential *causes* of disease, not the diseases themselves.

Preparation 2 (group)

In a group, compare and discuss your lists.

Now read the next part of the article (below) to see how accurate your guesses were.

Of the 10 risk factors, the five that dominate in poor countries are: abnormally low body weight, unsafe sex, iron deficiency, unsafe water and exposure to indoor smoke from solid fuels.

"Indoor air pollution was a complete surprise," says Christopher Murray, overall director of the report. The smoke causes pneumonia in children and lung disease in women.

In richer countries, the five key killers are tobacco, alcohol, high blood pressure, high blood cholesterol and obesity.

Murray says that a big surprise was the unexpectedly large impact of high blood pressure, cholesterol and alcohol on intermediate-level countries such as India and China.

"They've always been perceived as problems of high-income countries," says Murray. So countermeasures now, as countries industrialise, could have disproportionately large benefits in the future, he says.

(Abridged from) Coghlan, Andy. "WHO sets out world's deadly top 10." 30 October 2002. http://www.newscientist.com/news.jsp?id=ns99992987 (8 January 2004).

Discussion

'The WHO says that cheap remedies exist and that governments of all countries can do more to prevent unnecessary and premature death.' Your group should choose to focus on *either* poor *or* rich and intermediate-level countries.

1 Look carefully at the five major risk factors which the WHO identified for the category of country you have chosen. If time is short, choose just two or three factors. What countermeasures do you think should be adopted to reduce these risks?

2 Were you surprised by any of the five factors in your list? Why? Are there any other factors you would have expected to be included?

Discussion Point 2: Globesity

Preparation (individual)

The text on the next page is from a newspaper report on a major scientific conference. It highlights a problem referred to as 'globesity'. This is a new word, which you may not have come across.

Before you read the text, discuss what you think 'globesity' could mean.

Now read the text to find out what 'globesity' is, and then discuss the questions that follow.

Globesity: the modern epidemic that is fast becoming the biggest danger to world health

A very modern epidemic is spreading across the globe but this one is not caused by any conventional infectious agent.

It is a global epidemic of obesity and it is spreading at an alarming rate, from the industrialised countries in the west to the developing world where it often sits side by side with malnutrition.

"Globesity" is fast becoming more of a problem than famine and under-nutrition, and has now reached a point where it is becoming a serious threat to the health of every nation striving for economic development, scientists said yesterday.

The global "fat epidemic" is no longer the exclusive problem of rich countries and many poorer nations are now facing the double threat of some of its citizens being malnourished while others are seriously overweight, the American Association for the Advancement of Science was told.

A study for the World Health Organization has found obesity is now estimated to affect 18 per cent of the global population, an increase of 50 per cent over the past seven years, said Marquisa La Velle, a social anthropologist with the University of Rhode Island.

"We assume in developing nations that the problem is one of undernutrition rather than overnutrition," she said.

"What we discovered is that worldwide rates of obesity have increased to the points where many cultures and societies have both undernutrition and overnutrition. This puts a burden on the developing world that it can ill afford and we are looking at a situation in which increased disease and a decline in world health is inevitable."

For the first time, the number of overweight individuals in the world rivals those who are underweight, and the developing countries have seen some of the biggest increases.

A 1999 United Nations study identified the growing problem of obesity in all developing regions, even in countries where hunger exists.

In China, the number of overweight people jumped from less than 10 per cent to 15 per cent in just three years. In Brazil and Colombia, the figure hovers around 40 per cent, a level comparable to a number of European countries.

Even sub-Saharan Africa, where most of the world's hungry live, is seeing an increase in obesity, especially among urban women.

Connor, Steve. "Globesity: the modern epidemic that is fast becoming the biggest danger to world health." *Independent*, 18 February 2002.

Preparation (groups)

Work in small groups, and discuss the following questions.

1 Were you surprised by any of the information?
2 Why should obesity be a problem? What do you think the consequences are?
3 What do you think the reasons for the worldwide increase in obesity are? Why do you think it is affecting poor countries? Do you think obesity is increasing in your country?
4 Do you think anything can be done to reduce the problem? What people or organisations do you think could play a role in tackling 'globesity'? What should they do?

Discussion

1 The International Obesity Task Force (IOTF) works to raise awareness of the problem. Suppose that, as part of a worldwide consultation process, your group has been asked by the IOTF to form a 'focus group' to suggest ways in which the problem could be addressed in your country/countries.
2 Brainstorm some ideas for tackling obesity and agree on one strategy which your group will recommend to the IOTF to help reverse the spread of obesity. Specify *who* (people/organisations) should be responsible for implementing the strategy, *how* it would be achieved, and *which sectors of the population* would be affected.
3 After you have agreed on the details of your recommended strategy, choose one member of your group to report on your idea to the rest of the class.

PRESENTATION SKILLS
Using visual aids
What are visual aids?
A visual aid is anything which your audience can see, and which helps them to follow your spoken presentation, and keeps their attention and interest.

Types of visual aid
For some presentations, a large physical model of the topic being presented can be helpful for demonstration: for example, a skeleton in an anatomy seminar, or a model of a bridge in an engineering seminar. In others, if the audience is small, objects can be passed around: for example, pieces of rock in a geology seminar, or herb extracts to smell in an aromatherapy seminar. Visual aids of this kind certainly make a topic more vivid and interesting. But not all topics lend themselves to relevant *realia*, and sometimes the audience is too big to make them a practical option.

By far the most commonly used visual aids in seminar presentations are graphs, tables, charts, diagrams, text or photographs, projected on to a screen. Three common types of projection are:

1 **Overhead projectors and transparencies** (sometimes called *acetates* or *slides*). This is the simplest and cheapest form of projection, and transparencies can be quickly produced. It is therefore usually the best choice for small academic seminars. Transparencies can be handwritten and drawn with special coloured pens or, for a more professional appearance, they can be photocopied from printed text.

2 **Slide projectors and slides**. For many years these have been the standard mode of projection in scientific conferences and meetings. Slides are more versatile than overhead transparencies; they can show photographs of laboratory apparatus, for example, or microscopic structures. They also have more colour impact than overhead transparencies: transparencies must always have a clear background, whereas slides may have, for example, a blue background, with white or yellow text. The disadvantage of slides is the process of making them. Some presenters can make their own, but often they have to be produced in an audio-visual department. So the process takes more time – and maybe money.

3 **PowerPoint projection, using a laptop computer and data projector**. This mode of projection is now standard practice in all international and national scientific conferences. It is also rapidly becoming standard practice in conferences in the arts, humanities

and social sciences, though overhead projection is still used, particularly for smaller or more informal workshop sessions.

Although PowerPoint presentations now dominate the conference scene, not all academic departments can afford expensive data projection facilities. So slide projectors and overhead projectors still continue to be used in these settings.

Graphs, tables, charts, diagrams and text can, of course, be shown to the audience without projection. They can be written on blackboard, whiteboard or flip chart. The disadvantage of these simpler procedures is that time is wasted while the presenter writes (unless it has been possible to prepare the boards or flip chart beforehand), and also the feeling of contact between presenter and audience can be lost, because the presenter has to turn away from the audience in order to write. However, if there is no projection equipment available or if the electricity supply is unreliable, then using the board as a visual aid is much better than having no visual aid at all.

Effective visual aids

The key to effective visual aids is to remember the two essentials.

1 Visual aids must be VISUAL.
  - If possible, use pictures or diagrams or graphs, rather than text. Use simple clear graphs and tables, with not too many lines. Make sure they can be seen by the audience at the back of the room.
  - If you use text, use short clear lists, with not too many words. Use large clear print. Make sure it can be read by the audience at the back of the room.
  - The slides should be well laid out and attractive but not distractingly decorated.
  - Each visual aid should have a title, so that the audience know what they are looking at.
  - If you are using a graph, table or text taken from another source, remember to put the reference on your visual aid.

2 Visual aids must be AIDS.
  - The slide should show the *key* points that you want to make. You will add comments while you speak, but if the audience can see your main points, this will help them to follow what you are saying. Note that this means, for instance, that a table of data on a visual aid is likely to be different from a table of data in a published article. The table in an article usually contains a complete set of detailed data, and the accompanying text highlights important points from the table. But in a

presentation, the table is much simpler, with only key points in it, and the presenter expands on these, if necessary, when speaking.

- When you have finished talking about the content of a slide, don't keep the slide showing while you talk about the next point. This distracts the audience and is not helpful. Remove it or use a new slide.

For more advice on using specific types of visual aids, see Checklist 2 on visual aids on page 120.

Language signals for visual aids

When you are presenting, you will need to refer to your visual aids. Again, it is best to keep the signals simple: *here* and *this/these* are frequently used and effective signals.

Referring to slides: language signals

1 Introducing the slide

You can see here...
Here you can see...
If we look at this slide...
Here are the data from our questionnaire.
These are the comparative mortality rates.
This slide shows the comparative mortality rates.

2 Locating a point on a slide

On the left side...   *On the right here...*
At the top...   *At the bottom...*

Analysis

Whether you use a board, a flip chart, an overhead projector, slides or PowerPoint, the most common types of visual aid are tables, graphs, diagrams and text.

1 Tables

Tables must be very simple, so that the audience can immediately understand them, and then listen to your comments. If the table is too complex, they will probably concentrate on trying to interpret the table and will not hear what you are saying about it. Tables used as visual aids in presentations should have no more than four columns and six rows; and fewer is better.

Table 1 – Participants in the trial

	Drug A	Drug B
Asthmatic group	115	120
Normal group	112	125

2 Line graphs

Line graphs are used to show changes over time. They should also be kept simple, with one, two, or three lines. If there is more than one line, use different symbols for different lines. The label for the y-axis should be written horizontally, not vertically as in many journals. The reader can turn a journal sideways to read a vertical label, but the audience cannot do that with your visual aid.

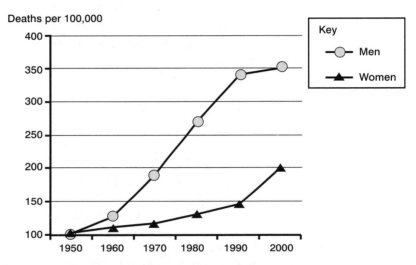

Figure 1 – Death rates for men and women (in a fictitious country) from 1950–2000

3 Bar charts, or graphs

Bar charts are one of the most effective ways of presenting data visually. They have visual impact, and most people understand them more quickly than they do tables and line graphs. They are used to compare any comparable categories of data. They may run vertically or horizontally. The bars should be the same width, and the space between bars or groups of bars should be at least half that width. To distinguish bars within a group, you can use shading, cross-hatching or colour.

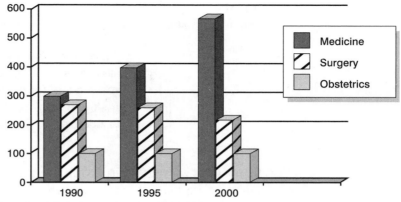

Figure 2 – Admissions to hospital 1990–2000

4 Pie charts

Pie charts are another extremely effective visual presentation of data. Their use is more limited than that of bar charts. They show what proportions make up a whole. Each part (or segment or slice) should be differentiated by shading, cross-hatching or colour, and should be labelled horizontally. Conventionally, the largest slice begins at the 12 o'clock position, then slices are sequenced clockwise in descending size. Use no more than six slices.

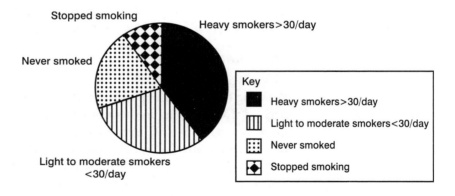

Figure 3 – Smoking status of patients in the study

5 Diagrams

Diagrams can be used to show processes, laboratory equipment, hierarchical categories and so on. An example of one kind of diagram, a flow chart, can be found on page 91 in Unit 6.

6 Text

When using text as a visual aid, follow these rules.

> **Text as a visual aid**
> - a bulleted list, not sentences
> - a separate line for each point
> - clear simple print
> - lower case letters, not capitals

What kind of visual aid would you use?

Discuss with two other students what would be the best kind of visual aid to use:

a) to show the route of the circulation of blood through the body

b) to compare the nutritional content of sugar and rice

c) to give the definition of two technical terms

d) to show the vaccination rates for different diseases in your country last year

e) to show the uptake of measles vaccination in your country from 1990 till now

f) to show the recommended percentages of carbohydrate, fat and protein for a healthy diet

g) to show the structure of the national health system in your country

h) to compare life expectancy for men and women aged 40

i) to compare life expectancy for men and women in 1960 and now.

Presentation practice

STAGE 1: PREPARATION

Working together with another student, make two visual aids derived from the data in the four tables on the next page (*Accidents in the Home*). It is NOT necessary to include all the data in the tables; in fact this would make bad visual aids. Discuss with your partner which data you want to select. Plan together what type of visual aids you will make. When you have planned both visual aids, decide who will make one and who the other.

Take a sheet of paper and make your visual aid.

Then plan how to describe it. Look again at the language signals for referring to visual aids on page 69. Plan how to phrase and emphasise your opening and final sentences. Be ready to give a *one-minute* presentation of your visual aid.

STAGE 2: PRACTICE

1 Speaking to the same partner, present your visual aid. They should take short notes of your main point or points.
2 When you have finished your talk, look at their notes. Have they understood your main point or points? Ask them if they found your visual aid helpful. Discuss what you should do to make your meaning clearer.
3 Then exchange roles with your partner.

Accidents in the Home

Patients who attended hospital following an accident at or near their homes were studied over a 12-month period to determine the factors which lead to such accidents. Information was obtained by examining the hospital records. Some of the results are given below.

Table 1 – Age (%)

infants (0–4)	14.1
children (5–9)	14.9
children (10–14)	14.2
adolescents (15–19)	8.3
adults (20–64)	37.8
elderly persons (65–84)	8.3
(> 85)	0.8
unknown	1.6

Table 2 – Place of accident (%)

kitchen	20.5
courtyard	18.3
bedroom	8.5
street	8.1
staircase	8.0
living room	6.5
bathroom	4.9
corridor	4.8
balcony	3.2
garage	1.7
other	14.5
unknown	1.0

Table 3 – Cause of accident (%)

falls		26.5
miscellaneous trauma		44.1
	knock	37.0
	sharp object	25.1
	burns	9.8
	electric tool	8.5
	bite	2.2
vehicle		24.7
unknown		4.7

STAGE 3: PRESENTATION

1 Now work with another pair of students. Show them your visual aids and give your talks.
2 Check afterwards whether the listeners' notes match what you intended to say. Ask them if the visual aids were clear. Did the visual aids make it easier for them to follow your talks?
3 Then exchange roles with the other pair.

STAGE 4: EVALUATION

What did you find when you heard the other students' presentations and saw their visual aids?

• Were they the same as yours or different? Had they selected the same points of content?
• Which do you think were the better visual aids, and why?

SUMMARY

Visual aids are an important part of a presentation because they:
• focus attention on key points
• help the audience to understand what you are saying
• provide visual interest to balance the spoken voice.

To be effective, visual aids should:
• be very simple and uncluttered, visually
• relate to the main points you are making, not the details
• be easy to read or understand at a glance.

UNIT 5 Environment

This unit aims to develop your speaking skills by:

1. improving your ability to interrupt appropriately in discussions
2. helping you to introduce your presentations effectively.

DISCUSSION SKILLS

Interrupting

Many international students report that one of the most difficult aspects of taking part in discussion with native speakers is getting the chance to say what they want to. In many English-speaking countries, academic discussion does <u>not</u> usually involve students politely taking turns to make their point, then quietly waiting for the next person to speak. In fact, tutorial or seminar discussion can sometimes seem quite competitive.

If you are in a group with confident speakers who are interested in the topic, you are likely to find that they don't leave many gaps in the discussion for you to contribute. It is quite usual in these situations for people to interrupt each other, and you may need to develop strategies to do the same if you want your voice to be heard.

Useful language

Some students worry because they don't know the polite expressions that they think they would need to interrupt without seeming rude and causing offence. In fact, native English speakers don't generally use elaborate or especially polite expressions to interrupt in this situation. As we saw in Unit 2, people usually express agreement or disagreement – even in an academic discussion – simply by beginning their comment with 'Yes,…' or 'But…'.

Interrupting

If you need to interrupt a lively discussion to get your chance to speak, it's a good idea to signal that you intend to interrupt before you make your point, for the practical reason that people may not hear you, or realise you are speaking, if you simply start to state your idea. The phrases people normally use to do this are quite simple.

Can I/Could I just say/ask…

If I could just say/ask…

I just wanted to say/ask…
Sorry, but I wanted to say/ask…

Delaying an interruption

If someone tries to interrupt <u>you</u> before you have finished making your point, you can try to make them wait.

Sorry, but if I could just finish what I was trying to say…
Could I just finish?

Re-taking your 'turn'

If your 'turn' is interrupted, you may want to go back to what you were saying before the interruption.

Yes, but what I wanted to say was…
What I was going to/about to say was…
Going back to what I was saying about…
As I was saying,…

Practice

For this activity, work in groups of four to six people, if possible. Your group should choose one of the following topics:

a) what you like best *or* least about this country
b) the best local shops (or restaurants/cafés)
c) your first memories of school
d) your favourite food.

You have to plan to speak about the topic for about a minute. Here are the instructions.

1 First spend a few moments planning what *you* want to say.
2 One member of your group should start to talk.
3 Listen carefully for an opportunity to add something *relevant*: you could agree or disagree with what the speaker has said, or you could describe an experience that relates to something they said. As soon as you spot an opportunity, try to *interrupt*, using one of the above signals, then continue talking as long as you can until someone else interrupts you. When you are interrupted, decide whether or not you want to finish your point. If you want to continue, use appropriate phrases from the above lists. When you get the chance, interrupt again.
4 Try not to let any one person speak for more than 5 or 10 seconds at a time! And speak as often as you can.
5 After *5 minutes*' discussion, your teacher will stop you.

Reflection

Briefly compare your answers to these questions.
- Did you manage to say everything you'd planned?
- How many times did you speak?

- Did you manage to delay unwanted interruptions?
- Did anyone speak more than the others?

Discussion point 1: Environmental problems
Preparation 1 (individual)
Read the following short reports on global environmental problems.

Global climate trends

The main drive behind climate change is the increasing amount of carbon dioxide in the atmosphere. Its level has risen by a third since the industrial revolution started in the 1760s. As CO_2 has built up, so temperature has risen. Over the past century, the Intergovernmental Panel on Climate Change estimates, the world warmed by 0.6°C. In this century, says the IPCC, we can expect temperatures to increase by as much as 6°C.

Warming oceans will expand, raising sea levels round the world. Some 50 million people a year already have to deal with flooding caused by storm surges. If the sea rises by half a metre, this number could double. A metre rise would inundate 1 per cent of Egypt's land, 6 per cent of the Netherlands and 17.5 per cent of Bangladesh. Only 20 per cent of the Marshall Islands would be left above water.

The main culprits behind increasing CO_2 levels are burning fossil fuels, farming practices, such as ploughing, and deforestation. We have already cut down more than half the forests that existed after the last ice age. Rich nations, such as those in North America and Europe, are now reforesting about 12,000 square kilometres a year, but in South America, Asia and sub-Saharan Africa, forests are still disappearing at 10 times this rate. The biggest factor behind rising CO_2 levels is burning fossil fuels. Countries such as the US and Australia emit more CO_2 per person than other nations because of their high dependence on fossil-fuel power plants and high living standards. The US alone pumps out a quarter of the world's CO_2 emissions.

[Sources: Deforestation, UNEP; Ecological footprint, Worldwide Fund for Nature; Global CO_2, temperature and sea level, IPCC; Energy and national CO_2 emissions, World Bank; Ozone, John Austin, Meteorological Office]

New Scientist. "Global climate trends." *Global Environment Report.*
http://www.newscientist.com/hottopics/climate/climatetrends.jsp (8 January 2004).

Global pollution trends

If car numbers keep increasing at the present rate, there will be more than a billion on the road by 2025. Today, motor vehicles put out 900 million tonnes of carbon dioxide a year – about 15 per cent of our total output. More vehicles will mean more global warming.

Also by 2025, two-thirds of the world's people will live in cities, so traffic jams and pollution will loom large in most people's lives. Worst of all will be the megacities of Asia. Beijing, Shanghai and Calcutta will each be home to as many as 20 million people, Bombay to 25 million.

Life in the country may not be much better. Asia is heading for a downpour of acid rain that will destroy forests and wither crops. The worst hit look like being Thailand, south-east China, north-east India and Korea, where economic growth is powered by fossil fuels rich in sulphur.

Industrialised nations have reduced SO_2 emissions. They have also cut production of CFCs and halons, the chemicals that destroy stratospheric ozone. But the ozone layer is not yet safe. Under the Montreal Protocol, developing nations have until 2010 to cut production. There is still a black market in CFCs, and halon production has increased in countries such as Brazil, India, Mexico and China.

[Sources: Vehicles, UNEP; SO2, CFCs and halons, World Resources Institute]

New Scientist. "Global pollution trends." *Global Environment Report.*
http://www.newscientist.com/hottopics/climate/climatetrends.jsp (8 January 2004).

Preparation 2 (individual)
Make a list of environmental problems facing the world. Include those mentioned in the text, and any others you know of. Which ones affect your own country?

Discussion
Form a group with three or four other students. If possible, your group should include people from different countries, or different regions in the same country. Discuss the following points.
1 Compare your lists of environmental problems, and add to your list any more that are mentioned by members of your group. Make sure everyone in your group understands all the problems listed.
2 Take turns to describe an environmental problem that affects your country or region. What are the causes and what is being done, or (in your view) should be done, to tackle them?

3 How serious a threat to the future of the world do you think environmental problems really are? Do you think technological advances and international cooperation will keep these problems under control, or are you more pessimistic about the future of the planet?

Discussion point 2: Traffic congestion

Preparation 1 (groups)

Increasing levels of road traffic is a problem affecting many cities and towns throughout the world. What problems does this cause?

Preparation 2 (individual)

Think about the following situation, and decide what *your* views are.

There is a serious and growing traffic congestion problem in the city where you are studying now, or the nearest big city. The city council has decided they must take action to reduce the problem. They propose to introduce a system of 'Congestion Charging'. This will mean that all drivers of motor vehicles (except for buses, taxis and emergency vehicles) will have to pay a substantial charge every time they drive into the city centre. The council say the income from the scheme will be used to improve public transport. The plan is controversial, because it will involve a large investment of public money to install special cameras and payment facilities, and because many people who say they need to use their cars for work object to the charges. Some owners of shops and small businesses in the city say it will threaten their livelihoods, but the council say they have been advised by experts that this is the only effective way to improve the traffic problem.

Discussion

You are local residents who have been invited by the city council to give your views on the Congestion Charge proposal.

1 Discuss your opinions about the proposal. Are you for or against? If you are against it, what do you think should be done to tackle the traffic problem?
2 If you can, you should try to reach agreement about your group's response to the proposal – but this may not be possible!
3 Your tutor will set a time limit for your discussion. When you have finished, choose one member of your group as a spokesperson to report your group's response to the rest of the class.

PRESENTATION SKILLS

Introducing your presentation

The functions of an introduction

The main functions of an introduction are to:

- catch the attention of the audience
- focus their attention on your topic and the objective of your presentation.

And often, though not always:

- to provide a framework for their listening by outlining your plan for the presentation.

If your presentation is at a conference, a programme will give your name and presentation topic, and a Chairperson (sometimes called Chair or Convenor) will introduce you and your presentation title. If so, then you will begin by thanking the Chair, then addressing the audience. If there is no Chair, then you will have to begin with a self-introduction. You may also want to acknowledge co-workers and your funding body. Here is an example.

Good morning, everyone.

My name is Karen Tang. I would like to talk to you today about the work I have been doing with my colleagues Bob Vogel and Anna Scarla, at the University of Proda. The research has been funded by the Worldwide Association of Pesticide Manufacturers.

If your presentation is at a departmental seminar, there is no need for you to be introduced. But you still need to catch the audience's attention and state your topic.

Normally an introduction will give some preview of what is to come. This could be very simple, as the example here shows.

There are three issues that I would like to discuss with you today.

Or the preview could be an outline of your presentation plan.

Before I tell you about our research, I would like to give you some background on how different governments have reacted to these problems. Then I will explain how these reactions have influenced the design of our study. After that I will take you through our results so far, and then will be happy to deal with any questions you may have.

If you would like your presentation to be interactive, this also should be stated in the introduction.

Please feel free to stop me at any time if you have a question or a comment.

Nerves and first impressions

Most people are nervous when they start their presentation, so the introduction is often the most difficult part of the presentation to perform. Unfortunately, the introduction is also important for setting the scene, not just in terms of your topic, but also in terms of your relationship with the audience. So if you begin your presentation very obviously nervous, and not fluent, this is a bad start.

It is important to think positively about your presentation. You have done the reading or the research, and you have prepared the presentation well. Everything is ready. The audience are waiting to listen to you, and are looking forward to being interested in what you have to say. Seminars can be a valuable opportunity for you yourself to learn more from the audience, through questions and discussion.

Accept that you feel nervous – everybody does to some extent – and use the extra adrenalin to give a strong performance. If you speak positively and confidently, then the audience relaxes and listens to what you have to say.

You should not, of course, sound over-confident and arrogant, as if you do not respect your audience. Nor should you be nervous and apologetic. Good advice is to think of your presentation as *sharing* knowledge – yours and the audience's.

Also good advice is to *prepare your introduction in detail*. Keep it simple. Do not memorise more than the first sentence, because that would add to the burden if you worry about forgetting it. But practise saying the whole introduction again and again, until it flows easily. Do not speak quickly. Speak slowly, with clear phrasing but no long silences.

If you practise well, then it will be much easier when you give the real presentation. Most people find that once they are under way with the main points, they feel much more at ease.

Analysis

Your teacher will play the first part of a presentation.

FIRST LISTENING

Listen and take notes. Don't worry about details, but note answers to these questions:

1 What is the topic of the presentation?
2 What are the main points that the speaker says she will deal with in her presentation?
3 Did the introduction contain any other feature typical of introductions?

Then compare your notes with those of another student. Do you agree?

SECOND LISTENING

Listen again to the talk, which the teacher will play in sections. Note the signpost and signalling phrases used by the speaker.

The speaker uses different verbs when announcing each point. It would be monotonous to say '*First I will tell you… Then I will tell you… After that I will tell you… Finally I will tell you…*'. It is useful to plan beforehand which verbs to use for signposting in your introduction.

Presentation practice

:········
: IELTS

STAGE 1: PREPARATION

Plan a talk (of about five to six minutes) on an environmental problem. The topic could be about rainforests, industrial pollution, disposal of nuclear waste, changing climate patterns, survival of game animals, traffic noise and pollution, building dams, litter in the streets – anything that you feel is important, and not getting sufficient attention.

Decide first what your main message will be. Then make an outline of your main points. (Look back to page 39 for suggestions on ways of organising the information in a presentation.) Make *very* short notes – just a word or two – under each of the headings:

• Introduction
• Main point 1 (plus example or comment)
• Main point 2 (plus example or comment)
• Conclusion

Decide which language signals you will use to introduce your main points and conclusion.

Then plan your Introduction section in more detail. Your introduction should be one to two minutes long. State your topic, then indicate the outline of your talk. Say that you will be happy to answer questions *during* your talk. You can use the signposting phrases that you heard in the recorded talk, or choose others from

Checklist 3 on page 122. Write out the first sentence and practise saying it firmly and clearly, with suitable phrasing and emphasis.

STAGE 2: PRESENTATION

Now give your presentation to two other students. They should pay particular attention to your introduction, and take note of its content. They should ask no questions during the introduction. They should make notes on these points:

- How did the speaker gain attention or greet the audience?
- Did the speaker state clearly the topic/objective of the presentation?
- Did the speaker give an outline of the structure of the presentation?
- Did the speaker say when questions could be asked?

As you continue with your presentation, they should then take notes of your main points. They should interrupt you **once** each, with a factual question (not an expression of opinion). Answer their questions politely but very briefly.

Then exchange roles.

STAGE 3: EVALUATION

1 Compare the notes you used in your talk with the ones the listeners took as you spoke. Did they understand all your main points? If not, discuss what you should do to make your meaning clearer.
2 Compare your notes on how you each introduced the talk. Did you miss anything from your introduction?
3 Ask them if they thought your style was appropriate. Was there any part of your talk that was too informal?
4 Ask them also if they thought your phrasing, emphasis and speed of delivery was appropriate. Would they advise any changes?

SUMMARY

1 The functions of an introduction are to:
- attract the attention of the audience
- introduce yourself, if necessary, and your topic
- focus the attention of the audience by providing an outline plan of the presentation
- state, if necessary, whether questions are welcome during the talk, or after
- establish a relationship between yourself and the audience.
2 You should expect to feel a little nervous at the start of a presentation. Keep your introduction simple, but prepare and practise it several times. You will then feel more confident when you do the presentation.

UNIT 6 Education

This unit aims to develop your speaking skills by:

1. improving the effectiveness of your questions
2. giving you practice in referring to visual aids during a presentation.

DISCUSSION SKILLS

Questioning

An important part of discussion is asking questions. In a seminar, there is normally time for questions and discussion following the presentation. You will also need to ask questions in less formal group discussion. In either situation, unclear or vague questioning can be problematic. For example, questions may be misunderstood if the point is lost in an over-long, unfocused sentence. One practical solution is to keep your questions short. Don't forget that, when you start to speak, you need to make clear whether you are asking a question or making a comment.

Confusion can also occur when it isn't clear *what* you are asking: for example, whether you are asking for more information, or just checking that you've understood what was said. You need to make clear:

1 that it's a question	*I have a question…*
2 what the topic is	*…about assessment:*
3 what the point is	*what is the balance between examinations and course work?*

Useful language

Introducing a question

> I've got a question about…
> Could I ask a question…?
> Sorry, could I just ask…?

Clarification

> Sorry, I didn't follow what you said about…?
> What did you mean when you said…?
> Could you give me an example of…?

More information

> I was interested in what you were saying about…

Could you tell us more about...?
Could you expand a bit on what you were saying about...?

Checking comprehension

So you mean...?
So you're saying...?
Can I just check I've understood – did you say...?
Have I got this right:...?

Responding to answers

A final aspect of questioning is how you respond to the answer you are given. It's important to let the person answering your question know whether their answer is satisfactory; for one thing, they need to know if they've said enough! If they have, it may be enough simply to nod, or you could say one of the following.

Yes, I see.
OK, thanks.
Thanks, that's clear now.

However, you may want to indicate that you are not satisfied with the answer.

That's not really what I was asking. What I meant was...
OK, but what I really wanted to know was...
Sorry, I'm still not clear about...
Perhaps I didn't make my question clear. What I was really asking was...

Practice

Work in small groups of four or five. *Without any preparation*, tell the others about your primary school. Each student should speak for no more than 60 seconds. Someone in the group should time each speaker, and stop them if they exceed the time limit. After each person has spoken, the others in the group should each ask *at least one question*. Use a different expression each time you ask a question.

Discussion point 1: Choosing a university/college

Preparation (individual)

1 Below are some of the criteria that may influence your choice of university or college. First, select which ones you will consider, or have already considered, in making your personal choice of institution. Delete any you don't consider relevant to you. Would you (did you) take any other factors into account? Add any other criteria to the list.

- Attractive city/town
- Convenient location for travel
- Cost of accommodation
- Cultural/recreational/sports facilities
- Entrance requirements (how easy to get a place)
- Friends/relatives studying there
- Good country to live in
- Good library and study facilities
- Good social life
- International reputation
- Local cost of living
- Modern teaching methods
- Recommended by friend
- Research expertise in your field
- Specific content of course
- Other factors: (state which)

2 Now rank your criteria in order of importance (1 = most important).

Discussion

Form a group with three to five other students. Agree on a list of five factors which you consider the most important in choosing a university/college to study at. You must agree on their order of importance.

If there is time after you have reached an agreement in your group, choose one member of your group to report your decision to the rest of the class. As a class, discuss the differences in your priorities.

Discussion point 2: Assessment

Preparation 1 (individual)

Read the following extract from a research report on international students' cultural misunderstandings about writing and assessment at a UK university.

False Expectations of Formal Requirements

Initially, students from different countries have widely differing expectations about even the *amount* of writing that will be demanded of them.

The survey of students in the University of Warwick indicated that 50 per cent had not expected to be assessed on the basis of written term assignments. They expected only to be assessed on the basis of examinations. Moreover, a majority of those interviewed reported that they had expected these examinations to be objective tests. In fact, written assignments are a compulsory part of all taught courses.

This problem comes very simply from the false expectation that educational structures and systems do not differ internationally. Students may believe that universities in Britain operate very similarly to their own country.

To illustrate the complexity of the problem, we would like first to consider one particular case of a student with writing problems. This student, whom we will call Nadia, entered a British university to study for a BA in Economics. She had previously successfully completed two years of a first degree in a university in her home country, largely through the medium of English. Although her spoken English is very good and she had an overall score on IELTS of 6.5 the previous September, she reported very serious problems with written assignments.

One of the questions in the questionnaire read as follows: Was there anything unexpected about the assignments in your department? (Try to explain in your own words.)

Nadia responded as follows: "Everything. First of all no written work was asked for in my home university."

In a subsequent interview, she reported that in her home university the assessment is by objective end-of-term examinations where the questions are multiple choice or short answer items. The questions are based on information from set books and lectures and require no interpretive or critical comment from the student. If you work hard and know the facts, you can do well. Writing skills are not required – at least at that level.

She has learned that things are very different in her present department. Here the students have to read academic papers reporting key experiments and write evaluative essays discussing methodology and applications and commenting on how to interpret the results. The game is not to show the assessor *that you know the facts* but to show the assessor *what you have read and, moreover, what you think about what you have read*.

Adapted from Bloor, Meriel and Thomas Bloor. "Cultural expectations and socio-pragmatic failure in academic writing." *Socio-Cultural Issues in English for Academic Purposes*. Eds P. Adams, B. Heaton and P. Howarth. London: Macmillan ELT, 1991: 1–2.

Preparation 2 (groups)

1 Discuss what you think the following expressions mean. If you aren't sure, ask your teacher.
   a) objective tests/examinations
   b) multiple-choice tests/examinations
   c) written tests/examinations
   d) oral tests/examinations
   e) written term assignments
   f) course work
   g) continual assessment
   h) practical work

2 Explain to the others in your group which of those assessment methods (above) you have experienced, or will experience, for the following purposes. Ignore any that do not apply to you. If some other method was or will be used, explain what it involves.
   A) at secondary/high school, to assess your progress
   B) for entrance to university
   C) on your undergraduate degree course
   D) on your postgraduate programme

If your answers included 'written tests/examinations', explain whether these involve *short* answers (such as single phrases/sentences) or *long* answers (such as essays). How much time were/will you typically be allowed for a long written answer? Ask questions if you need clarification or if you would like further information.

Discussion

Consider your views on the following questions, then get into a group to discuss them.

1 Are written examinations a good way to assess students? Discuss their advantages and disadvantages.
2 In assessing students on a university course, what percentage of the final mark (grade) should written examinations account for?
3 Should any other forms of assessment be used in addition to or instead of written exams?

PRESENTATION SKILLS
Referring to visual aids

In Unit 4 we considered different types of visual aids and their function. We also looked briefly at language signals referring to visual aids. However, speakers have to do more than simply refer to visual aids (*here are the data,* a*t the top you can see,* etc.). They have to speak about the visual aids, expanding text on text slides, for example, and adding more information to any slide. The visual aid acts as the main framework and reference point for what the speaker says.

Look again at this text slide example from Unit 4.

> **Text as a visual aid**
> - a bulleted list, not sentences
> - a separate line for each point
> - clear simple print
> - lower case letters, not capitals

If you were presenting this slide, you could not just read it out. You should say something like this:

> When you are preparing a text slide, all these points are important.
> First, you should never put whole sentences and long stretches of text on a slide. It is better to use a bulleted list, as we have here.
> Second, don't try to get more on the slide by putting two points together. Whether you use bullet points or not, there should always be a separate line for a separate point – one point, one line.
> The next thing to remember may seem obvious, but it is amazing how often one has the experience in the audience of not being able to read a visual aid because the letters are too small! So use very large print that everyone can read. Font size 22 or 24 is usually good.
> And research has shown that people find lower case letters easier to read than capitals.

Clearly, you could not put all that text on a visual aid.

Sometimes, speakers who are not confident about their English put too much text on their visual aids and then read the text aloud. This is not good practice because:

- the visual aid has too much on it, so the print has to be too small, and it is difficult to read
- even with too much text, there is not the amount that one would normally use to expand on headings (see the example above), so much is lost from the spoken presentation

- it is boring for the audience, and has no purpose or advantage. Why sit and listen to the speaker reading something they could read themselves?

It is better to make clear simple visual aids (graphs, diagrams or *short* text) and practise speaking about them, putting into words the information shown in graphs and diagrams, and expanding short text. The visual aid is useful to the speaker as well as the audience, providing a framework for what to say and a sense of security. With practice, you should become able and confident.

If you still do not feel confident, you could take additional short notes with you. PowerPoint can produce pages showing your slides in miniature and space beside them for notes, or you can hand-write on paper copies of your visual aids, or write separate short notes on A5 size paper or card. In practice, this can complicate the process of presenting because you have slides, notes and the audience to attend to. Usually, repeated practice is the better option.

Analysis

Study the visual aid below (Figure 1). It is from an overhead transparency. Working with a partner, decide on its meaning and expand on the text. Try speaking about the slide to each other. Then the teacher may ask you to present the slide to the class.

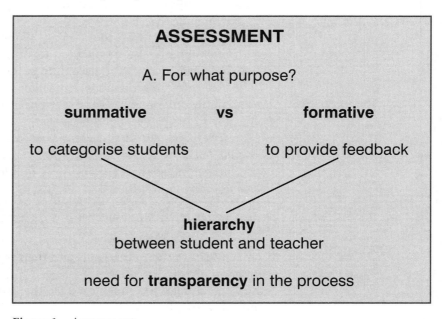

Figure 1 – Assessment

You will now hear a recording of the presentation where this visual aid was used. The speaker also used a flow chart (Figure 2, below)

FIRST LISTENING

1 Looking at Figures 1 and 2, listen and take notes on the main points.
2 Then compare your notes with those of another student. Do you agree?
3 How helpful did you find the visual aids? Would you have understood the talk as easily without them?
4 Did you find one visual aid more helpful than the other? How would you evaluate the two visual aids? Do you think they could be improved?

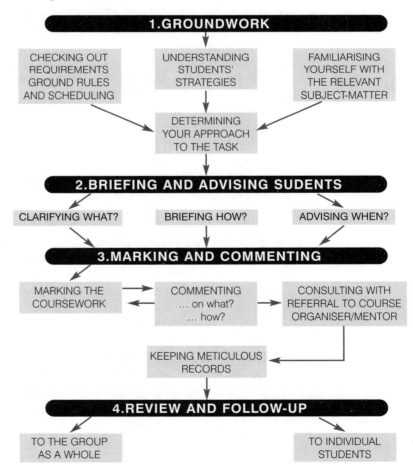

Figure 2 – Assessment, marking and feedback

SECOND LISTENING

Listen again to the talk, which the teacher will play in sections. Note the signalling phrases the speaker uses to focus the audience's attention on different visual aids and on specific parts of visual aids. Notice also how she expands on the text in the visual aids.

Presentation practice

IELTS

STAGE 1: PREPARATION

Plan a talk (of about five to six minutes) on any aspect of education that interests you. You can choose a topic either related to the texts in the *Discussion skills* section of this Unit or to the talk you have just listened to, or you can choose something different, for example: changes in teaching methods over the last twenty years; the importance of nursery education for child development; the benefits of self-directed learning as opposed to attending classes all day; or the advantages and disadvantages of using unqualified teachers in a literacy programme.

After you have chosen your topic, decide what your main message will be. Then make an outline of your main points. (You can refer back to Unit 1 for suggestions on ways of organising the information.) Make *very* short notes – just a word or two – under each of the headings:

- Introduction
- Main point 1 (plus example or comment)
- Main point 2 (plus example or comment)
- Conclusion

Make two visual aids, one for each of your main points. You can use a diagram, a picture or text. Think about what you will say relating to each visual aid. Decide which language signals you will use to introduce all sections of your talk. In your introduction, say that there will be time for questions after your presentation.

STAGE 2: PRESENTATION

Working with two other students, give your presentation, showing your visual aids when appropriate. They should take notes. After the presentation, they should ask you one or two questions, which you should answer politely and briefly. Try to keep the question and answer style in fairly formal academic English, like the presentation. (Imagine there are 100 other people in the room listening.)

Then exchange roles.

STAGE 3: EVALUATION

1 Compare the notes you used in your talk with the ones the listeners took as you spoke. Did they understand all your main points? If not, discuss what you should do to make your meaning clearer.

2 Discuss each other's visual aids critically. Were they effective and clear? Could they be improved?

3 Consider: Were there any parts in your talk when you did not have a visual aid but wished you did have? Were there any points that you had difficulty expressing, even though you had a visual aid? If so, discuss these together and decide on what would be the best way of handling the content and the visual aids.

SUMMARY

- Do not read aloud text on visual aids.
- Visual aids should be simple and clear, showing key points.
- Put into words the information given graphically.
- Expand on the information given in text slides.
- A good visual aid provides a useful framework for you as well as the audience.
- If you need more support, you could take additional short notes.
- Practise speaking to your visual aids, again and again, and you will become more fluent and confident.

UNIT 7 Culture

This unit aims to develop your speaking skills by:

1. improving the way you report ideas in discussions
2. helping you conclude your presentations effectively.

DISCUSSION SKILLS

Reporting

In seminar or tutorial discussion, you often have to talk not only about your own ideas, but also those of the authorities in your field that you have read in textbooks and journals or heard about in lectures. You have to take care to make it very clear to your listeners when you are expressing your <u>own</u> opinions, and when you are <u>reporting</u> ideas you have read or heard about. (The same is true when you write.)

Useful language

> X says...
> According to X,...
> X defines...as...
> X describes...as...
> X believes...
> X's theory is that...
> X argues that...
> X makes a strong case for...
> X suggests that...

Note: Use just the *surname* (or personal name and surname), of the authority you are referring to – *not* titles such as Doctor or Professor.

> According to Sen,.../Sen argues...
> According to Amartya Sen,.../Amartya Sen argues...

Critical evaluation

Of course, you are expected to read and understand the key literature on the topic you are studying. But, as we pointed out in Unit 6, in the Western academic tradition it is not enough just to *know* the ideas: you are also expected to show that you can *evaluate them critically*. This means being able to form your own informed opinions about them.

The verb *claim* is very useful when you want to show that you do <u>not</u> necessarily accept the ideas you are reporting. When you say:

X claims that...

your listeners will understand that you have doubts about the validity or truth of the idea.

To express your critical evaluation more directly, you can use the same vocabulary that you use to express opinions generally (see also *Useful language* in Unit 1).

I think X is right about...
X is quite right when he/she says...
I'm not sure I accept X's point about...
I'm not sure I'm convinced by X's argument that...
I don't agree with X about...
I can't accept X's idea that...
X doesn't produce any evidence for his/her claim that...

You normally use the **Present Simple** tense when referring to people's ideas in discussion.

X says (not *X said*)...

But when you report research findings, use the **Past Simple**.

X found that...

Practice

Work in a group of three or four people. Spend a few minutes reading the following ideas and data. Think about how you could <u>report</u> the material. Do you have an opinion about it? If so, think about how you could express that.

Take turns to practise reporting each item. Each student in the group should try to find a different way to report each one. If appropriate, let your listeners know your opinion.

Note: When you report ideas in discussion, you would not normally read out the exact words from your source material. It is more usual to summarise or paraphrase the ideas in your own words. Try not just to read out of the book – focus on getting *the main idea* across clearly.

1 'We have global markets but we do not have a global society. And we cannot build a global society without taking into account moral considerations.' (George Soros)
2 Number of TV sets per 1000 people in East Asia
   1985: **50**
   1995: **250**
   (World Bank)

3 'The relative risk of breast cancer increased by 7.1% for each additional 10g per day intake of alcohol, i.e. for each extra unit or drink of alcohol consumed on a daily basis…. These results suggest that about 4% of the breast cancers in developed countries are attributable to alcohol…. Smoking has little or no independent effect on the risk of developing breast cancer.' (Cancer Research UK)

4 'There needs to be greater recognition that what is called Western science drew on a world heritage, on the basis of sharing ideas that made science what it is.' (Amartya Sen)

5 'If we win the battle with nature, we'll end up on the losing side.' (E.F. Schumacher)

6 'Cloning…will probably come to be accepted as a reproductive tool if it is carefully controlled.' (Robert Edwards)

Discussion point 1: Coping with cultural differences

Preparation 1 (individual)

One of the predictable difficulties you can expect to encounter when you go to a different country to study or work is language. But difficulties may also result from cultural differences, which are often less obvious at first, and can be unexpected. Your teacher will ask you to read a definition of one of two terms: *culture shock* or *culture bumps*. Prepare to report the meaning of the term you have read about to another student.

Preparation 2 (pairs)

Work with a student who has read the other definition.

1 Take turns to explain to each other the meanings of the terms you have read about. Don't read out the definition you have read, but explain what your term means using your own words. What is the difference between the two phenomena?

2 Tell your partner about any experience you have had (or heard about) of:
  a) a **culture bump**. Was it negative, neutral or positive?
  b) **culture shock**. Did you overcome it? If so, how? How long did the process take?

Discussion

Now form a larger group of four to six students. If there are students from different countries in your class, arrange your groups so that you have a mixture of nationalities in each group.

1 Describe any experiences you (or your partner in the last activity) have had of culture shock or culture bumps.

2 Your group has been asked to write a leaflet giving advice to foreign students coming to study at the institution you are studying at on how to avoid culture shock. What difficulties do you think a foreign student might have adapting to life in this country? How could these be minimised?
You must agree on five main points that should be included in the leaflet.

3 When you have decided on the advice you will offer, choose someone in your group to report your group's decision to the rest of the class.

Discussion point 2: Hofstede's dimensions
The dimensions of national culture

You are going to read part of a summary of an influential theory of cultural diversity, proposed by Geert Hofstede[1], a Dutch academic. Hofstede's work was originally intended to improve intercultural understanding in the business world (it was based on research into the IBM corporation), but it has also been applied in other fields.

Hofstede devised a framework for analysing national cultures based on four dimensions: 'power distance', 'individualism/ collectivism', 'masculinity/femininity' and 'uncertainty avoidance'.

Preparation (individual)

Your teacher will ask you to read a short explanation of one of Hofstede's dimensions. You will be asked to <u>report</u> what you have read to two or three students who have not read your text. Read your summary carefully, using a dictionary if necessary, and plan how to explain the information to your group. You can make notes if you like, but don't write out a 'script'.

Discussion

Your teacher will organise you into groups of three or four students who have each read about a different 'dimension' of Hofstede's cultural framework.

1 Take turns to explain what you have read to the other students in your group. You must not just read out your text! Use your own words. Remember that at this stage you are simply <u>reporting</u> what you have read, not giving your own views. Check that you have made yourself clear, and try to answer any questions you are asked.

[1] Hofstede, G. *Culture's Consequences: International Differences in Work-Related Values.* London: Sage, 1980.

2 Listen carefully to the other students' reports on their readings, and *make notes* on the key points. Ask for clarification of any points you haven't understood.

3 Here are some points to discuss – but feel free to add more:
   - Can you apply Hofstede's analysis to your own national culture? Try to rate it 'high', 'medium' or 'low' on each of Hofstede's dimensions.
   - If you have experience of another culture, how would you define it on the four dimensions?
   - Do you think this kind of analysis could help people of different cultures understand each other better?
   - Do you have any criticisms of this approach?
   - One criticism that has been made of Hofstede's theory is that it seems to imply that cultures are fixed and unchanging. Do you think your national culture is changing? If so, can that change be described on Hofstede's dimensions? Which one(s)? Do you think that change is a good thing, or not? Explain your answer.

TEXT 1A

'Culture shock', by H. Douglas Brown

Culture shock is a common experience for a person learning a second language in a second culture. Culture shock refers to phenomena ranging from mild irritability to deep psychological panic and crisis. Culture shock is associated with feelings in the learner of estrangement, anger, hostility, indecision, frustration, unhappiness, sadness, loneliness, homesickness, and even physical illness. The person undergoing culture shock views his new world out of resentment, and alternates between being angry at others for not understanding him, and being filled with self-pity.

(Abridged from) Brown, H. Douglas. *Principles of Language Learning and Teaching.*
Englewood Cliffs, NJ: Prentice Hall, 1980: 28.

TEXT 1B

'Culture bumps', by Carol M. Archer

Certain situations (e.g., arriving late for class) exist in all but a few cultures, and each culture develops particular responses that are labeled "polite" for these situations: for example, North American culture teaches university students who are late for class to enter quietly without knocking and sit down, while Chinese culture teaches university students to knock, offer an explanation, and wait for the teacher's permission to enter. A culture bump occurs when an individual has expectations of one behavior and gets something completely different. The unexpected behavior can be negative or neutral or positive. Unlike culture shock, which extends over an extended period of time, culture bumps are instantaneous, usually over within minutes or even seconds, though the effect may be long-lasting, and can occur any time one is in contact with members of a different culture.

(Abridged from) Archer, Carol M. "Culture bump and beyond." *Culture Bound*. Ed. J. Valdes. London: Cambridge University Press, 1986: 171.

TEXT 2A

Power distance

Power distance is defined by Hofstede as 'the extent to which the less powerful members of institutions and organisations within a country expect and accept that power is distributed unequally'.

In nations with a low power distance, such as the United Kingdom, inequalities among people will tend to be minimised, decentralisation of activities is more likely, subordinates will expect to be consulted by superiors, and privileges and status symbols are less evident. In high power-distance nations, conversely, inequalities among people are considered desirable, there is greater reliance by the less powerful on those who hold power, centralisation is more normal, and subordinates are likely to be separated from their bosses by wide differentials in salary, privileges, and status symbols.

TEXT 2B

Individualism/collectivism: behaviour towards the group

'Individualism pertains to societies in which the ties between individuals are loose: everyone is expected to look after himself or herself and his or her immediate family. Collectivism as its opposite pertains to societies in which people from birth onwards are integrated into strong, cohesive in-groups, which throughout people's lifetime continue to protect them in exchange for unquestioning loyalty.'

In some societies, people need to belong to a group and have a loyalty to the group. Children learn to say 'we'. This is true of countries such as Japan, India and China. In other societies, such as the United Kingdom, individualism is more important, and there is a lower emphasis on loyalty and protection. Children learn to say 'I'. In strong collectivist countries, there tend to be greater expectations of the employer's obligations towards the employee and his or her family.

TEXT 2C

Masculinity/femininity: behaviour according to gender

'Masculinity pertains to societies in which social gender roles are clearly distinct; femininity pertains to societies in which the social gender roles overlap.'

In a masculine society (Hofstede gives the United Kingdom as an example), there is a division of labour in which the more assertive tasks are given to men. There is a stress on academic success, competition, and achievement in careers. In a feminine society such as France (according to Hofstede), there is a stress on relationships, compromise, life skills, and social performance.

The last 10 to 15 years have seen enormous changes – a 'feminisation' process – in the behaviour of Western democracies. It has also been said that the emergence of developing countries is as much about feminisation as it is about dealing with harder business and economic realities.

TEXT 2D

Uncertainty avoidance: the need for structure

Uncertainty is 'the extent to which the members of a culture feel threatened by uncertain or unknown situations'.

In some societies, there is a pronounced need for structure. This is because those societies tend to fear the unknown and to possess a high degree of uncertainty. Countries characterised by a low level of uncertainty (such as the United Kingdom) do not perceive something different to be dangerous, whereas, in strong uncertainty-avoidance societies, people will seek to reduce their exposure to the unknown and limit risk by imposing rules and systems to bring about order and coherence. The same thing can be seen in organisations: for example, where there is a need for rules and dependence there will tend to be a pyramidal organisational structure.

Business. London: Bloomsbury, 2002: 1004–5. (Quotations from Hofstede, Geert. *Cultures and Organisations: Software of the Mind.* Maidenhead: McGraw-Hill, 1991.)

PRESENTATION SKILLS
Concluding your presentation

The importance of a firm clear conclusion

In Unit 6 we said that how you present your Introduction is important because it makes a first impression. Similarly, the delivery of the Conclusion is important because it leaves a final impression which can colour, retrospectively, the audience's view of your entire presentation. It leaves a bad general impression if you stop your presentation awkwardly, or rush through your final points because of lack of time, or, even worse, have to stop your presentation before you reach the conclusion. In fact the conclusion is so important, that if you find you have mistimed your presentation and it is going to be too long, then you should omit your last main points or summarise them in a sentence, and go straight to the conclusion.

The conclusion is also important from a practical point of view, in that it offers the opportunity for a summary of your main message, so if the audience has not followed parts of your presentation this can be redeemed in the conclusion.

A conclusion should always be delivered firmly and strongly, usually at a slightly slower pace than the main body of the presentation. Keep the content brief and to the point, but don't rush the ending.

Signalling the conclusion

Start your conclusion with a language signal.

Signals for concluding

In conclusion, In summary
To conclude, To sum up, To summarise
So
Finally

Signal the last sentence of the conclusion by your delivery. Catch the attention of the audience by lowering your voice slightly, slowing the pace, and using shorter phrasing and more emphasis. Then do not just stop, or mumble: *That's it* or *That's all I have to say* or *I've finished now.* Instead, pause briefly, smile at the audience, and say firmly: *Thank you.* If there is no-one in the Chair, you might then want to say: *Are there any questions?*

If you are using an overhead projector, switch it off before you ask for questions. A PowerPoint presentation should be left running – with a final blank slide showing – in case you need to return quickly to a slide during question-time.

Content of the conclusion

Most conclusions consist of a summary of the main points of the presentation, perhaps highlighting any point that is particularly important. Most lectures and course seminar presentations end in this way.

Sometimes, recommendations are made in the conclusion. For example, the presentation in Unit 5, about organic farming and the environment, ended with a series of recommendations (not shown in this book).

If the presentation is of your own research, the conclusion may include some evaluation of your study. You can:
- relate the findings to your original hypothesis
- comment on the methods and how these affected the findings
- indicate the application of your findings, either in practical 'real life' or to the development of theory
- make recommendations for further research.

Analysis

You will hear the concluding part of a seminar presentation.

FIRST LISTENING

Listen and take notes. Do not worry about details, but answer the questions below.

Your teacher will play the recording section by section, stopping after the answer to each question. Discuss your answer with another student, then check with the teacher.

1 The speaker re-states the main research question, in general terms. What was the topic of the paper?
2 The speaker reminds the audience of the *two* sets of data that the researchers considered. What were they?
3 The speaker emphasises that the main conclusion of the paper is to recommend further research with a more rigorous methodology. What *three* factors have to be taken into consideration?
4 The speaker indicates what the main finding seems to be so far. What was it?

SECOND LISTENING

Listen again to the talk.

a) Notice that the speaker says *we* and not *I*. This is because she is representing a group of researchers.
b) As you listen, note the verbs (and verb phrases) that the speaker uses to report academic investigation. For example, she begins by saying 'so in this paper we've *evaluated* a number of arguments'.

Presentation practice

STAGE 1: PREPARATION

Plan a talk (of about 5 to 6 minutes) on the influence of American English and North American culture in your own country.

Decide first what your main message will be. Then make an outline of your main points. (See Unit 1, page 39 for suggestions on ways of organising the information in a presentation.) Make *very* short notes – just a word or two – under each of the headings:

- Introduction
- Main point 1 (plus example or comment)
- Main point 2 (plus example or comment)
- Main point 3 (plus example or comment)
- Conclusion

Decide which language signals you will use to introduce all the sections of your talk.

Then plan your conclusion in more detail. You should summarise the main points, and perhaps highlight the most important, or suggest a recommendation, or make a prediction. The conclusion should be brief – for a 5–6 minute talk a conclusion should be **half a minute to one minute** long.

Look at the verbs and verb phrases you noted in the Analysis section. Plan to use at least three or four of them.

Write out your last sentence, and practise speaking it slowly, firmly, with short phrasing, and emphasis. Remember to add the end signal *Thank you*.

Questions should be kept till after all three talks have been given.

STAGE 2: PRESENTATION

Now give your presentation to two other students. One listener should time your talk, and tell you when you have spoken for nearly 5 minutes. If you have not started on your conclusion by then, you should move on to it immediately. The listeners should take notes of your main points while you are speaking and also note answers to the following.

1 Did the speaker use a language signal at the start of the conclusion?
2 Did the speaker summarise their main points clearly and briefly?
3 Did the speaker use a slightly lower voice, change of pace, and effective phrasing and emphasis in the final sentence?
4 Did the speaker remember to pause, look at the audience and smile, and say *Thank you* at the end?

Then exchange roles.

STAGE 3: EVALUATION

1 Compare your speaking notes with the ones the listeners took as you spoke. Did they understand all your main points? If not, discuss what you should do to make your meaning clearer.

2 Compare your notes on how you each concluded the talk. Did you forget to do anything?

3 Ask them if they thought your style was appropriate. Was there any part of your talk that was too informal?

SUMMARY
- Your presentation should have a strong firm conclusion.
- Even if you have to hurry some of your main points in the body of the talk, don't hurry the conclusion.
- The conclusion should normally contain a summary of the points in your presentation.
- The conclusion may highlight a point that is especially important.
- It may include a recommendation.
- It should be brief.
- The last sentence should have weight; it could sum up your main message.
- Give the last sentence weight by speaking firmly, with a lower voice and slower pace, short phrases and clear emphasis.
- Conclude gracefully by saying *Thank you* to your audience.

UNIT 8 Globalisation

This unit aims to develop your speaking skills by:
- 1 improving your skill in dealing with questions
- 2 helping you make your presentations more interesting.

DISCUSSION SKILLS

Dealing with questions

People sometimes feel nervous about having to answer questions. You may feel your knowledge or understanding is being tested. For example, students who are preparing to give a presentation sometimes worry more about being asked 'awkward questions' than about the presentation itself.

If you can answer a question directly, you don't need to use any special language or techniques; you just explain what the facts are or give your opinion. The simple words 'OK,…', 'Right,…', 'Well,…' are clear signals that you have understood the question and are going to answer.

Useful language

Below are some other phrases that can begin a straightforward answer.

Answering directly

Well, as I understand it…
If I've understood X correctly,…
Well, according to our results…
OK – I think I can answer that quite simply…

'Playing for time'

You may need a few moments to organise your thoughts before you give your answer. Some cultures tolerate more <u>silence</u> in conversations than others. In most English-speaking cultures, you are expected to respond to a question almost immediately. If you don't say something straight away, people may think you have not heard or cannot answer, and you may lose your chance to speak. But you can create a little thinking time by prefacing your answer with a 'delaying' phrase.

Er, let me see…
Well, I suppose I'd say…
That's an interesting/a very good question! Well,…

Handling complex questions

You may have to organise your answer to questions that are more complex than they seem.

Well, those are really two different questions.

OK – let me deal with those questions one at a time. Your first question /point was about…

I'll deal with your second question/point first, if I may.

Dealing with awkward questions

However, it is not always easy to answer a question, for a number of reasons. One reason is that you may not understand the question! We looked at how to ask for clarification in Unit 6. Below are some more reasons why you may find it difficult to give a satisfactory response to a question. Can you think of any others?

Why questions can be awkward

A **You don't know the answer.**

B **The question implies some criticism of your argument/research/understanding etc.**

C **The questioner has misunderstood the issue.**

D **The question cannot be answered simply or briefly.**

E **You don't think the question is relevant to the discussion.**

F **You want to finish talking about something else before you deal with the question.**

Exercise

Below are expressions that can be used in dealing with awkward questions. Working with a partner, try to match each expression with one of the reasons (A–F) above.

1 *I take it you don't think/believe/accept…?*
2 *I don't really have any experience of that, but X might like to comment?*
3 *I don't think there's enough evidence to say for sure.*
4 *I haven't had time to look into that, sorry.*
5 *I really don't know.*
6 *I think we should stick to the main issue here.*
7 *I think we're going off the point a little.*
8 *I was just coming to that…*
9 *I'll come back to that in a minute, if that's all right. I just wanted to…*
10 *I'm not (quite) sure.*
11 *I'm not absolutely sure, but I'd guess that…*
12 *I'd need to think about that.*
13 *I've really no idea.*
14 *That isn't really my field, but perhaps X could say something about…?*

15 *That's an important question, but it's really too complex to deal with now.*

16 *That's rather out of my field.*

17 *That's really a whole different argument/discussion/topic.*

18 *There isn't really time to go into that now/here.*

19 *Well, I think you'd be wrong to assume that…*

20 *You seem to be assuming that…*

Look again at the expressions you matched with **Reason A** – *You don't know the answer*. Can you subdivide those expressions under these possible reasons for not knowing the answer? (Some may be suitable for more than one reason.)

a) **You have not thought about the issue before.**

b) **You have not read or remembered the information.**

c) **The question has not been researched, or the research is inconclusive.**

d) **The question is outside your specialism.**

You may nevertheless want to suggest an answer, even if you are not sure of the facts.

Well, just off the top of my head, I'd say…

Well, my gut feeling is that…

I can't be sure, but I'd be very surprised if it wasn't…

Can you explain the meaning of *off the top of my head*? What is a *gut feeling*?

Avoiding an answer

We've seen that you can avoid answering a question that is irrelevant, or that would take too long to answer. Another strategy to avoid giving an immediate answer is to offer to check later.

I'm afraid I can't give you an answer off the top of my head. Can I get back to you on that?

A final avoidance strategy is to answer a question with a question!

Can I ask what's behind your question?

Well, what's your own view?

Why do you ask?

Practice

In small groups, ask each other awkward questions! Here are some examples.

What's the population of Finland?

How quickly are global temperatures going to rise?

Will alternatives to petrol-driven cars be successful?

How many words are there in your first language?

Try to begin answering each question quickly. Choose a different expression to answer each time.

Discussion point 1: What does globalisation mean to you?
Preparation 1 (individual)
Read the following text.

> Globalisation is the result of unprecedented scientific and technological advances. Microchips, jet planes, satellites and optical fibres are among the key inventions that have made a fast-moving, interlinked word possible. Over the past decade the costs of computing, telecommunications and transport have plummeted. Combining these technological changes with the opening of markets to the free passage of goods and finance has led to a huge boom in world trade, rapid economic growth with all its fearsome consequences for the environment, high-speed global financial markets and the dominance of a Western culture based on consumerism and individualism.
>
> "The Chips are Down." *New Scientist.* 27 April 2002: 30.

Preparation 2 (individual)[1]
Think about what you understand by the word 'globalisation'. What aspects of life are affected by globalisation? What have been your own personal experiences of globalisation? Think of any events, incidents, advertisements, trends, changes in your way of life or anything else which have represented 'globalisation' to you in your own country.

Discussion
Now compare and discuss your experiences of 'globalisation'. How similar have they been?

Discussion point 2: The causes and effects of globalisation
Preparation 1 (individual)
Your teacher will ask you to read one of four texts. They are excerpts from a lecture given in 1999 by Professor Anthony Giddens, Director of the London School of Economics. Prepare to report the main ideas to other students who have not read the text. Make notes on the key points, but don't write a 'script' to read out.

---

[1] This task is adapted from an activity designed by Dr Michael Northcott, University of Edinburgh.

Preparation 2 (individual)

This time, it is up to *you* to devise the discussion questions! You should think of two questions on the topic of globalisation that you think it would be interesting to discuss. Your first question should be related to the ideas in the lecture excerpt you read (for example, you could find out whether other students agree with one of Giddens's points). Your second question can be on any aspect of globalisation that interests you.

Write down your questions. Try to make sure the questions are expressed clearly and correctly.

Discussion 1

Now form a group with students who have read different excerpts from Professor Giddens's lecture.

1 Take turns to report the main ideas of the excerpts you have read to the others in your group. Don't read out the texts, but summarise them informally in your own words. Pay special attention to how you deal with *questions*. Try to use appropriate expressions.

2 As you listen to the other students' reports, make notes on the main ideas. You must try to ensure that you *all* understand the key ideas in all the texts. If you are not sure if you have understood a point, ask for clarification.

Discussion 2

Start with the questions related to the lecture extracts. One person should read out their question, and check it has been understood by the whole group. The group should discuss the question as fully as possible (the teacher may set a time limit). Try to contribute something to the discussion of each of the questions. When you are ready, take another question, and continue until everyone's first question has been discussed. If a question is very similar to a previous one, skip it and move to the next person.

When all the first questions have been discussed, discuss the other questions in the same way.

TEXT 1

Origins of globalisation

I would like to propose to you that it's a basic mistake to treat globalisation as solely or even primarily economic. The economic marketplace is certainly one of the driving agencies of intensifying globalisation, but globalisation is not primarily economic. Globalisation refers to a set of changes, not a single dimensional change. Many of these changes are social, cultural and political, rather than purely economic, and one of the main drivers in addition to the global marketplace is something partly separable from it, which is the communications revolution. I think the late 1960s is the time at which the revolution in electronic communications started to transform both the ways in which we're able to relate to one another across the world and also the inner content of economic systems. I say the late 1960s because that was the first time at which a satellite system was sent up above the Earth. Originally it was a non-commercial satellite system – commercial satellite systems date from the early 1970s.

Once you have a network of communications satellites in place it means you can communicate from any part of the Earth to another and, at least in principle, instantaneous global communication is possible. To me this has changed an enormous amount about world society, and it has also changed a great deal about our personal lives too. It's changed a lot in world society because when you have instantaneous communication in which television and other electronic media are the leading agencies it invades the texture of our experience. It changes aspects of sovereignty and politics and these are very visible. It's not too much to say that the decline and the fall of the Soviet Union was bound up with these transformations. The Soviet Union was able to survive pretty well in the old industrial world and it built itself on hard industry: factories with big chimneys and heavy industry was its core. It kept up with the West pretty well in terms of growth rates until the early 1970s. The Soviet Union started to fall behind after that period because it couldn't compete in the new global electronic economy and because its system of authoritarian top down power was not compatible with the softer forms of power which function more effectively in a globalised communications system.

TEXT 2

Globalisation and self-identity

Globalisation is not just about 'out there' phenomena, it's not just about the big systems, it's not just about the global marketplace, it's not just about processes affecting states. It's an 'in here' phenomenon too. Our lives, our personalities, our identities, our emotions, our relationships with other people – these are being reshaped by globalising processes, because globalisation invades local culture. Increasingly tradition and custom are declining in their impact on our lives. Even in the more traditional cultures this is true. As they do so, you face much more of an open future. Facing an open future means creating a self-identity rather than simply taking self-identity from a cultural background or traditional form of history. This is a process which is liberating, it has many emancipatory consequences, but it's also frightening. Personally, I think women are caught up in this paradox and this puzzle most forcefully of all, because the changes affecting women's lives are affecting them very radically. To be a woman used to mean domestic life, to have children, to be largely subordinate in a male dominated universe. It still means many of these things but they have radically changed. Women are much freer in a western country than they were a generation ago, but what do you do with that freedom? How do you live, how should you look, how should you relate to other people? Will you marry? For the first time ever you have the situation where many women in western countries say they do not want to have children. 25 per cent of women under 30 in EU countries say seriously that they do not intend to have children, and the birth rate in some EU countries is down to about 1.1 to 1.2, which is the lowest birth rate ever known in any society in human history. Women have to make sense of these things and of course as they do so the position of men starts to change very radically too.

TEXT 3

Globalisation and the nation-state

I think it's plain that writers who argue the nation state is disappearing are wrong. The nation state is still a vital power in the world. In some ways you could say that in the global era, the nation state is even more rather than less important than in the past. The reason I say this is that until very recently other alternatives to the nation state existed. For example, the Soviet Union was a kind of empire, it was a form of imperial system. Empires have existed at various points in the twentieth century prior to the present time. All formal empires with the possible exception of the American Empire, if you want to call it that, have disappeared from the world. All nations have become nation states, so that's a big transformation. You could say this is the first time in which the nation state has actually become a near universal form. You couldn't say the nation state is disappearing in this sense. Moreover, nation states remain more important than their chief power rivals in the global system, the large corporations. Exxon, for example, is one of the biggest corporations in the world. Its revenue over the year is larger than all but about 9 or 10 of the world's nations. Such gigantic corporations are globalised enterprises. However, it seems to me that these big companies are not as powerful as nations, certainly not as powerful as the larger nations. The reasons are that nations still have territory, whereas companies don't. Nations still have access to military power and control the means of violence, whereas corporations, if they ever do, only do so very obliquely. Nations are still largely responsible for establishing frameworks of law, and those frameworks of law substantially affect what corporations can do in the world.

TEXT 4

Globalisation and the dominance of the West

Is it all a western plot? Is the expansion of globalisation simply an expansion of western power which is corrupting, destroying traditional cultures, and enforcing the dominance of the West over the rest? Well, briefly put, you have to recognise that globalisation is dominated by western powers. Most of the big corporations are located in the West. The United States is still, or has easily become the dominant super power, and is in a position to shape the world economy according to its own interests. All these things, I think, have to be accepted. The world system is heavily skewed in power towards the West, and within the West the United States is the dominant economic, political and military power. This said, I think it is quite false to draw from this the conclusion that globalisation is simply a western phenomenon. That is false. Globalisation is much more complicated, much more decentered, and much less within our control than such a view would suggest. Globalisation affects every country in the West just as much as every other country in the world and globalisation has many positive benefits to offer. It is a mistake to suppose that globalisation is at the origins of increasing economic inequalities in the world. It is a mistake to suppose that a kind of protectionist opting out of globalisation processes would help the poorer countries.

(Abridged from) Giddens, Anthony. "Runaway World: the Reith Lectures revisited. Lecture 1: Globalisation." *The Director's Lectures*, 10 November 1999. http://www.lse.ac.uk/Giddens/pdf/10-Nov-99.pdf (8 January 2004).

PRESENTATION SKILLS
Making it interesting

Content is important. Some presentations are certain to be interesting, because they report a news-breaking discovery. Presentations of badly designed research studies with unclear results cannot be made interesting. But if the content is at neither of these two extremes, there is a lot you can do to make it more interesting – or less! So for many presentations, content matters, but how you present it also matters.

No-one wants to give a boring presentation. So what can you do to make your presentation more interesting?

1 Appropriate objectives and precisely defined message

The first priority is to be sure that your selection of content is relevant to your audience's interests and appropriate to their level of knowledge. You should also know yourself what you are talking about! And you should have a clear idea of what precisely the main message of your presentation is.

2 Clarity of communication

The second priority is to make sure that you deliver your message clearly. If the audience cannot follow your presentation, how can they find it interesting? A clear presentation is, in itself, a pleasure to listen to.

In the other units of this book we have considered many different ways – all important – of making your message clear.

Make the overall structure of your presentation clear to the listeners
Do this by:
- preparing a logical planned outline of main points
- stating the precise topic clearly at the start
- giving a preview of the outline in the introduction
- signalling when you move from point to point in the outline
- summarising your main points in the conclusion.

Make your points clear as you speak
Do this by:
- giving examples
- using visual aids
- using language signals, indicating examples, contrast, additional points, and so on
- grouping words into meaningful units
- using your voice for emphasis of selected points.

3 Making it vivid

After the first two priorities (clarity of message and communication) have been met, then you can think of ways of making your presentation even more interesting.

You can do this by:

- providing surprising statistics
- telling a personal anecdote
- giving vivid examples related to everyone's experience
- suggesting an analogy not from your subject field
- quoting from a famous author.

Techniques like these are sometimes recommended for attracting the audience's attention at the start of a presentation. We think that this is more appropriate for an after-dinner speech or a marketing presentation. As a general rule, a simple clear start is advisable for academic presentations.

Research has shown that audiences' attention is actually highest at the beginning of a presentation, then it dips, and then it increases again when they hear the signal for the conclusion. Vivid techniques are therefore usefully placed in the middle, to keep attention. Or, if you can find something appropriate to your message, they can be used to special effect as a dramatic last sentence.

Analysis

Your teacher will play a recording of a four-minute talk on globalisation.

FIRST LISTENING

Listen and take notes on the main points.

Compare your notes with those of another student. Do you agree?

SECOND LISTENING

Look again at the techniques for making a presentation more vivid (see 3 above). Can you remember any instances of these in the talk? Working with a partner, note any you can remember.

Then listen again to check, and to add to your list.

Presentation practice

STAGE 1: PREPARATION

Choose one of the aspects of globalisation that were mentioned in the talk. Plan a talk about it (of about five to six minutes).

Decide first what your main message will be. Then make an outline of your main points. Make *very* short notes – just a few words – under each of the headings:

- Introduction
- Main point 1 (plus example or comment)
- Main point 2 (plus example or comment)
- Main point 3 (plus example or comment)
- Conclusion

Think of at least one way to make the talk more interesting: through example, anecdote or quotation. Add this to your outline.

Plan your introduction and conclusion in detail. Write the first sentence of the introduction and the last sentence of the conclusion, then practise saying them with suitable phrasing and emphasis. Decide which language signals you will use to introduce all the sections of your talk. If you have time, you could make simple visual aids. Be ready to answer questions after your talk.

STAGE 2: PRESENTATION

1 Now give your presentation to two other students. They should take notes of your main points. One should time your talk, and let you know when you have spoken for nearly five minutes. If you have not started on your conclusion by then, you should move on to it immediately.
2 After your talk, invite questions, and deal with them.
3 Now exchange roles and repeat.

STAGE 3: EVALUATION

1 Compare the notes you used in your talk with the ones the listeners took as you spoke. Did they understand all your main points? If not, discuss what you should do to make your meaning clearer.
2 Ask the other students if they found your talk interesting. Can they suggest any ways that you could have made it more interesting?
3 How did you evaluate your performance yourself? Think of:
   a) content
   b) focused message
   c) structure

d) signalling points

e) phrasing and emphasis

f) appropriate style

g) introduction

h) use of visual aids or notes

i) conclusion

j) dealing with questions.

What do you think you did best? What do you feel most needs improvement?

Discuss your self-evaluation with the other two students to see if they agree.

SUMMARY

For an interesting presentation, you must have:
- well-chosen content
- a well-structured plan
- clear delivery.

To make your presentation even more interesting, you can include one or more of the following:
- surprising statistics
- a personal anecdote
- examples related to everyone's experience
- an analogy not from your subject field
- a quote from a famous author.

PART 3

Class seminars

Overview

Part 3 of the course consists of a series of seminars on topics chosen by the members of the class. Everyone will get the chance to lead a seminar, which lasts 30 minutes of class time:
- 10 minutes **to give the presentation**
- 10 minutes for **audience questions and discussion**
- 10 minutes for **feedback** from tutor and students.

These materials will guide you through three stages of work on your seminar: Planning – Rehearsal – Presentation.

Planning
For this stage, follow the advice in Checklists 1–3 (pages 119–123).

Rehearsal
The most effective way to rehearse is to record yourself as you practise giving your presentation. When you rehearse the presentation, you should stand up using your notes and your visual aids exactly as you will be doing at the seminar.

Before you do the rehearsal, read through Checklist 4 on *Non-verbal communication* (pages 123–124). Think about the points mentioned there.

Apart from the obvious benefits of practice, one main advantage of rehearsing is that it allows you to time your presentation. However, bear in mind that it often takes about 20 per cent longer to talk 'live' to an audience than in the rehearsal, so for a 10-minute presentation, you should aim to speak for about 8 minutes in rehearsal.

Listen carefully to the recording. If you can ask someone else to listen to the cassette and tell you where they didn't understand, so much the better. Note the points you need to improve. Record yourself again. The more often you can practise, the more successful the final result.

Giving the presentation
The audience will want to ask questions and to raise points to discuss with you. Think about the probable questions and discussion points before you give the presentation. Look through Checklist 5 on *Asking and dealing with questions* (pages 125–126).

When you are dealing with the questions, be **patient** with the questioners! If they ask about something you mentioned in the presentation, that means you did not make the point clearly enough. Be **positive**. If they have questions to ask or points to make, it shows they are interested in the topic you have chosen to speak about.

Don't forget to repeat or summarise the question, in order to make sure you (and the audience) have got it right – and to give yourself a little longer to think about your answer.

Checklist 1 PREPARING A PRESENTATION

STEP 1	Know the context of the presentation: Who are the audience, and what are their interests? How big will the audience be? How long is the presentation to be? What facilities are available for visual aids? What about time for questions?
STEP 2	Decide on your topic. Think carefully about the main point or points that you want to communicate. You should be able to write these clearly in one or two sentences.
STEP 3	Structure the content. Most people begin with an unordered collection of ideas and then put them into sequence. Then decide on the relative weight of each section of the talk.
STEP 4	Think of ways of catching the listeners' interest: examples, anecdotes, impressive statistics, interesting quotations.
STEP 5	It is useful to 'rough-draft' visual aids at this stage, because they can help you make the sequence of points more clear and logical. Think about whether some information should be put into handouts.
STEP 6	Check overall length, and the relative weight of sections. A little too short is better than even a little too long. As a rough guide, allow about 1 minute for every 100 words, plus time if necessary for changing transparencies. One A4 page, double-spaced, takes about 3 minutes of speaking time.
STEP 7	Finish preparation of visual aids. If you are using PowerPoint data projection, having slides or transparencies available is a useful back-up in case of last-minute technical problems.
STEP 8	Prepare handouts, if you want them. Make copies.
STEP 9	Plan the exact words you will use for the opening, the transition points, and the conclusion. Practise them again and again. If you are anxious, write on cards the introductory and concluding sentences. Make more notes if you need them (see Checklist 2).

STEP 10 REHEARSE your presentation, as often as necessary. Do not omit this step! You can practise alone, or ask a friend or colleagues to listen to you. With practice, you will become more fluent and at ease. Make sure you speak simply, but in academic not conversational style. Project your voice across the room. You will find this slows your speech. Check the timing carefully and make adjustments if necessary. Mark a time reference at one or two points in the presentation.

STEP 11 Think about the questions the audience may want to ask you. Plan how you will answer them.

STEP 12 On the day of your presentation, be calm and organised. If you are unfamiliar with the location, go beforehand to plan where you will stand and where you will put your papers and to see how the projection works. Arrive in good time for your presentation. Remember to take all your visual aids, notes and papers.

If you feel nervous, do not worry. That's normal. Breathe slowly and deeply for a few minutes beforehand, and try to relax the muscles of your face, mouth and neck. This will make you look relaxed, and will improve the quality of your voice. Then remind yourself how well prepared you are, and enjoy it. Concentrate not on yourself or your notes, but on the audience and making clear to them what you have to say.

Checklist 2 USING VISUAL AIDS, HANDOUTS and NOTES

See Part 2, Units 4 and 6 for general advice on visual aids.

VISUAL AIDS If you are using an **overhead projector**, follow steps 1–4 below.
1 Before your presentation check that the equipment works. Decide on the best place to stand, so that you do not obscure the view of the audience; decide where to put transparencies before and after use; decide whether you will point at the transparency or at the screen (or not at all).
2 If you point at the transparency, use a pen as a pointer.
Detach the transparencies from their backing paper to make things easier during your presentation. Interleave them with plain paper.
4 Number the transparencies in case you drop them.

If you are using **PowerPoint** data projection, follow steps 1–6 below.
1 Check beforehand whether you should bring your presentation on diskette or CD or DVD. If you are bringing a computer, check on the type of connection required for the data projector.
2 If possible, set up your presentation before your talk. This can take several minutes, even if all goes well.
3 Have a blank slide at the start and end of your presentation. This makes your start and finish smooth.

4 PowerPoint has an excellent online tutorial and help system. Use it when you are preparing your presentation so that you can make full use of its facilities (such as time monitoring, handouts and notes).

5 Don't be tempted, because of PowerPoint's capabilities, to make your slides too 'busy'. That will distract the audience's attention.

6 Even if you are giving your presentation in a well-equipped room, technology can go wrong. Print out your PowerPoint slides on to transparencies, so that you have an alternative.

HANDOUTS   Handouts are useful in three ways.

1 They show data that are too detailed for a visual aid, such as transcript data from interviews, or mathematical calculations. If there is a lot of detail, the points you want to refer to in your presentation should be clearly highlighted in the handout. The handout is given immediately before the presentation, and then referred to.

2 They provide a 'signposting' framework to guide the audience through your talk. In this case, the handout will be a note-frame, which is given out before the presentation. Don't put too much into it, or the audience will read the handout instead of listening to you.

3 They act as a record of your presentation, which the audience can take away. This could be either a note-frame or a fuller text. For this 'record' type of handout, it's common practice to add your address and email address, so that people working in the same field can contact you later. Some presenters like to give out this type of handout at the end of their talk, so that the audience listens with full attention. Others give it out at the start, as a support to listening.

Keep your handout short – one page if possible.

NOTES   Visual aids often provide sufficient support for your presentation. If you feel you need notes as well, remember that they will be more to cope with during the presentation: you will have to deal with the visual aids, the notes, and the audience.

1 Cards or A5 paper are often recommended because they are neater in the hand than big pages. Make sure you number them clearly!

2 A good alternative is to use photocopies of your visual aids, with notes written on them. It is then easier to coordinate your progress through notes and visual aids.

3 Write very large and clear, with plenty of space.

4 Use colour, so that you can quickly locate key points or words.

Checklist 3 SIGNPOSTS AND LANGUAGE SIGNALS

INTRODUCING THE TALK	*I'd like to*	*talk about...*	
	I'm going to	*discuss...*	
	I want to	*tell you about...*	
	What I'd like to do	*is*	*to explain to you...*
	What I'm going to do	*is*	*to describe...*
	What I want to do	*is*	*to give an account of...*

ORDERING POINTS (TIME ORDER)	*To begin with*	*At the beginning*	*At the start*
	Second(ly),	*Then Next After that*	
	Finally,	*At the end*	

ORDERING POINTS (LISTING AND ADDING)	*First(ly),*	*Second(ly),*	*Third(ly),*
		A second reason	*The third aspect*
		Another point	*Other factors*
		Also	*In addition*
		Last(ly)	*Finally*

STARTING A NEW SECTION	*Now*		
	Moving on to	*If we move on to*	*I'd like to move on to*
	Turning to	*If we turn to*	*I'd like to turn to*
	What...?	*Why...? How...?*	*Which...?*

TRANSITION	*Having considered (X), let us now move on to (Y).*
	So these were our methods. What about our results?

CONTRASTING	*But However*	*Nevertheless,*
	On the other hand	*By contrast*

REFERRING TO VISUAL AIDS	*This slide (graph, chart) shows...*		
	Here you can see	*Here are*	*This is*

DEFINING	*By X we mean yy.*	*We call X yy.*
	X is defined as yy.	*We can define X as yy.*

REPHRASING	*That is, In other words, To put it another way,*

GIVING AN EXAMPLE	*For example,*	*For instance,*
	such as say, like including	
	To give you an example,	*An example of this is...*
	Let me give you an example.	*Here is an example.*

EMPHASISING	*Actually* *in fact* *indeed*
	Importantly *surprisingly* *interestingly*
	It is clear that *clearly* *obviously*
	I'd like to underline *highlight* *emphasise* *stress*
	It's important to bear in mind *keep in mind* *remember*
CONCLUDING A SECTION	*So*
CONCLUDING THE TALK	*So* *Finally,*
	To summarise *Summing up* *To conclude* *In conclusion*
	I'd like to finish by saying...
	I'd like to conclude now with a few remarks about...

Checklist 4 NON-VERBAL COMMUNICATION

POSTURE

a) Stand straight but not stiff.

b) Balance your weight evenly on both feet.

c) Standing well allows your diaphragm to move more easily to control your breathing and voice production. So you feel better, sound better, and look better.

MOVEMENT AND GESTURES

a) Too much movement is distracting; no movement at all is boring and uncommunicative.

b) Use movements and gestures to signal transition points or to stress points of importance.

c) Avoid meaningless gestures and repetitive movements. Don't wave your left hand about in circles or wave the pointer about. Use the pointer only when necessary, and with a firm movement. If you have a laser pointer, keep your hand close to your body when using it; don't hold it at arm's length like a gun.

FACIAL EXPRESSION

a) Your facial expression must match your message. If you claim something is interesting, look as if you find it so.

b) Relax your facial muscles. If you look nervous, the audience will not be comfortable.

c) In the 10 minutes before you start, make sure your tongue is relaxed and not raised tensely against the roof of your mouth. If you can discreetly yawn widely once or twice, this will help to relax your facial and throat muscles and to feel less tense.

VOICE	a) Speak a little louder than you think is necessary. Project your voice to the back of the room. Use your diaphragm to do this, not the muscles of your throat. Keep the muscles of your throat and mouth relaxed. Otherwise your voice loses resonance and power, and is less pleasant to listen to.
	b) Speak a little more slowly than you normally do, especially if you feel nervous. This will help you sound and feel more confident. A useful rule-of-thumb is: the larger the audience, the more slowly you should speak.
	c) Use your voice as a communication tool. Vary the speed – speak more slowly in the introduction and the conclusion. Use stress for important points and contrasts. A short silence can also serve to emphasise a point or a transition. All these techniques contribute greatly to making a presentation interesting to listen to.
EYE CONTACT	a) Eye contact creates a relationship between the speaker and the audience. It encourages the audience to listen. It helps to relax the speaker. So look at people.
	b) Start and end with direct eye contact, looking round the whole audience. During the talk, don't gaze over people's heads or out of the window. Look at your visual aids (and notes if you have them) as much as is necessary, but don't stare at them and talk to them. Look at the audience as much as you can.
	c) Don't look always at the same section of the audience or, even worse, at one 'victim'. Don't dart your eyes about quickly or sweep your gaze round like a searchlight. Focus on one person or group for 1–2 seconds; then look at another person or group, then another.

Checklist 5 ASKING AND DEALING WITH QUESTIONS

ASKING QUESTIONS

GENERAL	Make clear:
	• that it's a question *I have a question*
	• what the topic is *…about assessment:*
	• what the point is... *what's the balance between exams and projects?*
INTRODUCING A QUESTION	*I've got a question about…* *Could I ask a question…?* *Sorry, could I just ask…?*
CLARIFICATION	*Sorry, I didn't follow what you said about…* *What did you mean when you said…?* *Could you give me an example of…?*
MORE INFORMATION	*I was interested in what you were saying about…* *Could you tell us more about…?* *Could you expand a bit on what you were saying about…?*
CHECKING COMPREHENSION	*So you mean…?* *So you're saying…?* *Can I just check I've understood – did you say…?* *Have I got this right:…?*
RESPONDING TO ANSWERS	*Yes, I see.* *OK, thanks.* *Thanks, that's clear now.* *That's not really what I was asking. What I meant was…* *OK, but what I really wanted to know was…* *Sorry, I'm still not clear about…* *Perhaps I didn't make my question clear. What I was really asking was…*

DEALING WITH QUESTIONS

ANSWERING DIRECTLY	Well, *as I understand it…* *If I've understood X correctly,…* *Well, according to our results…* *OK – I think I can answer that quite simply…*
'PLAYING FOR TIME'	*Er, let me see…Well, I suppose I'd say…* *That's an interesting/a very good question! Well,…*
HANDLING COMPLEX QUESTIONS	*Well, those are really two different questions.* *OK – let me deal with those questions one at a time.* *Your first question/point was about…* *I'll deal with your second question/point first, if I may.*
DEALING WITH AWKWARD QUESTIONS	*I haven't had time to look into that, sorry.* *I really don't know/I'm not (quite) sure/I've really no idea.* *I'd need to think about that.* *I'm not absolutely sure, but I'd guess that…* *I don't really have any experience of that, but X might like to comment?* *I don't think there's enough evidence to say for sure.* *I was just coming to that/I'll come back to that in a minute, if that's all right. I just wanted to…* *That's rather outside my field.* *That isn't really my field, but perhaps X could say something about…?* *That's an important question, but it's really too complex to deal with now.* *That's really a whole different argument/discussion/topic.* *There isn't really time to go into that now/here.* *I think we're going off the point a little.* *Well, I think you'd be wrong to assume that…* *You seem to be assuming that…* *Do I take it you don't think/believe/accept…?*

PART 4

Strategies for success

Improving your speaking outside class

It's time to think about how to continue to improve your spoken English after you have completed this course. In this final section we look at ways of getting independent practice and feedback in your daily use of English, when you no longer have access to a class and teacher.

We will be dealing with the following issues
- What makes speaking difficult?
- Conversation: Problem-solving strategies
- Pronunciation
- Grammar and vocabulary
- Fluency
- Feedback

What makes speaking difficult?

Precisely what makes speaking difficult depends what we mean by 'speaking'. The word covers a wide range of activities, such as:
- chatting with friends
- sorting out a problem over accommodation
- returning a faulty CD player to a shop
- calling an office to arrange insurance
- participating in a tutorial
- asking directions in the street
- giving a seminar presentation.

The difficulties arising in those situations are not only to do with language; some situations would also be difficult in our first language. When doing those things using English, it is important to analyse exactly what the source of difficulty is. Below are comments from four international students, who were interviewed during the first term of their degree courses at Edinburgh.

Discussion task 1

All the students mention their problems in speaking English; and most also suggest possible reasons. Underline the problems and circle the reasons. Then compare your answers with others' in your class.

1 I find myself not having much chance to speak. I believe I have fairly good skills in writing and reading but when it comes to speaking, I realise I have a lot of problems in expressing myself. When I speak Italian, I know I do it beautifully because I am very much conscious of using grammatical sentences and the right words. I want to do the same with my English. However, because there are differences in the grammar between the languages, I am

sometimes confused and make a mess of my English sentences as I tend to think in Italian.

2 Pronunciation is my main problem. I think I do all right in my grammar and vocabulary gives me some problems as well. I think the English phonetic system should be taught in Hong Kong.

3 In Taiwan I was more confident in speaking because among Taiwanese my English is considered to be fairly good. However, when I came here, I lost confidence in speaking and because of different accents I have problems in listening as well. I believe confidence is very important in speaking.

4 I have very little vocabulary so I can't really express myself. I don't have problems in grammar or other skills. My main problem is lack of vocabulary and I think inadequate knowledge of the English phrasal verbs is also a communication barrier.

(adapted from Luk 1994: 395–6)

Conversation: Problem-solving strategies

One reason why conversation is such a complex activity in another language is that it requires both speaking and listening skills. When communication becomes difficult, we have to adopt strategies to solve the problem. Which strategy we use depends whether the problem arises with the speaker or the listener.

When the speaker doesn't know a word – or can't remember it – they need to find another way of expressing the desired meaning. For example, if you were the speaker you could:

- use a more general word, such as *animal* instead of *shrew*
- describe the appearance or function of the thing you want to talk about, for example *in a portable bed – the one that the hospitals use to carry people that have had an accident*
- invent a new word made up of words you already know, such as *keymaker* for *locksmith*
- show the meaning by using your hands, for example by clapping to show *applause*
- ask the other person for help, saying, for example, *What do you call…?*

When the listener doesn't understand (or hear), they need to signal the problem, so that the speaker and listener together can resolve the difficulty in one of the following ways.

As listener you can:

- indicate that you have not heard
- indicate where the problem lies
- ask the speaker to repeat what they said

- ask the speaker to explain what they meant
- repeat what you think the speaker said
- ask the speaker to slow down.

As speaker you can:
- repeat what you said
- clarify what you meant
- go back to a point earlier in the conversation
- speak slower and more clearly
- check whether the listener has now understood you.

Practice task 1

Think of something that is specific to your home country or home region – for example, a sport, festival or tradition. Describe it to another student who is unfamiliar with it. When you have to mention a special term, explain it as precisely as possible in English. If communication problems arise, use the list of strategies in this section to help you sort them out.

Pronunciation

Many students believe that the cause of their problems in speaking English is their pronunciation of certain sounds that are difficult for speakers of their first language. Examples of these sounds would include the l / r distinction for speakers of Chinese and Japanese, and the voiced th / z difference for speakers of French.

One of the students we quoted at the start of this section said he thought he should have been taught the symbols of the English phonetic system in Hong Kong. Here is a similar comment from a Spanish student.

I think the phonetic symbols are very useful. My problem is that I never learnt how to use them, or how to pronounce the words with them. You have to know the real differences between the sounds, especially the vowels. Even if I know the sounds in my ear, it would help to read them from the page.

(Anderson and Lynch 1996: 117)

Knowing the symbols certainly helps you to learn the correct pronunciation of a new word when you look it up. Dictionaries contain a guide explaining which sound each symbol represents, with words illustrating each sound. However, if you find that the differences between the sounds of those example words are not clear to you as you read them (for example, the symbols used to differentiate *low* from *law*), then you could ask someone to help; of course, if you have a CD dictionary, that will allow you to hear the word pronounced.

But in real-life communication the pronunciation of individual sounds matters much less than <u>the correct placement of stress within words</u>. If you pronounce the sounds of a word reasonably accurately but put the main stress on the wrong syllable, you may still be misunderstood. Again, use your dictionary to find out and learn where the main stress should be in new words as you encounter them. You should also listen carefully to the way you hear people stressing a new word.

Practice task 2

Here are eight words from the previous paragraph. Work with another student and take it in turns to say the words as you think they should be stressed. Underline the syllable that you think receives the main stress.

ILLUSTRATING   COMPETENT   EFFECTIVE   INDIVIDUAL SYLLABLE   ACCURATE   MISUNDERSTOOD   ENCOUNTER

Check your answers with a dictionary or with the teacher.

Grammar and vocabulary

Two of the students we quoted earlier picked out grammar and vocabulary as reasons for their relatively weak spoken English. Here again is what they said.

I have very little vocabulary so I can't really express myself. I don't have problems in grammar or other skills. My main problem is lack of vocabulary and I think inadequate knowledge of the English phrasal verbs is also a communication barrier.

I find myself not having much chance to speak. I believe I have fairly good skills in writing and reading but when it comes to speaking, I realise I have a lot of problems in expressing myself. When I speak Italian, I know I do it beautifully because I am very much conscious of using grammatical sentences and the right words. I want to do the same with my English. However, because there are differences in the grammar between the languages, I am sometimes confused and make a mess of my English sentences as I tend to think in Italian.

Discussion task 2

Which of those students do you think had the more serious problem?

The two students were describing different types of problem. The first student's problem is more basic. He simply did not know enough words in English; as he himself put it, his weakness was a *lack of vocabulary*. The solution is to find ways of increasing his stock of words.

The second student must have had quite a good *passive vocabulary* because he described himself as fairly good at reading. ('Passive vocabulary' is a slightly old-fashioned term these days; current alternatives include *sight vocabulary, receptive vocabulary* and *recognition vocabulary*.) The student was able to recognise words in reading but was unable to find the appropriate words and grammar when expressing himself in English. What he needed to do was to access his existing vocabulary and grammar quickly when speaking. In other words, he needed to become a more fluent speaker of English.

Below are suggestions for various strategies to address the students' different problems.

Strategies for increasing your vocabulary and grammar

- Read as much general English as you can (newspapers, magazines, the Net).
- Listen as much as possible to English TV and radio.
- Make your own lists of words you recognise as important.
- Check the words' meanings and grammar in the dictionary.
- Note as much information about them as you can (for example, translation, synonyms in English, grammar, syllable stress).

You could also use the *Academic Word List* (Coxhead 2000). This is a list of roughly 600 keywords (word families), which commonly occur in academic texts across all disciplines. Recognising the various members of the word families will help you when reading and listening in your field. It is available at http://www.vuw.ac.nz/lals/div1/awl/

A very useful website for work on vocabulary is the *Compleat Lexical Tutor* at the University of Quebec: http://132.208.224.131/

Strategies for fluency

Keep an audio diary

Fix a regular time each evening to spend 5 minutes recording yourself talking about the events of your day. Try to imagine you are talking to one particular person, rather than to the microphone. Don't prepare in advance what you are going to say. When you have finished, rewind and listen to the recording, stopping at any parts where you had pronunciation difficulties or weren't sure about the syllable stress or couldn't find the exact word. Check those points in a dictionary – or if possible with someone else – and then re-record those parts.

Analyse other speakers' fluency

Videotape TV programmes in which people are involved in discussion. As you replay the video, look and listen for the signals by which the speakers indicate that they want to speak next, or are about to finish what they are saying. Make a note of any useful phrases the speakers use to emphasise their current point, for example *as a matter of fact* and *that may have been true in the past, but….* Try to use them in your audio diary the next day.

Rehearse short talks

For some types of speaking, such as giving a presentation, it is possible to prepare in advance. Here is a suggestion from another of our past students at Edinburgh.

I talk aloud to myself to prepare for a seminar. I do it at least twice – once aloud and once quietly. Sometimes if you are thinking, you may have to stop and think of a word, so I practise to get more fluent. I don't worry about pronunciation, except some key terms.

(Anderson and Lynch 1996: 122)

Practise speaking under time pressure

When we are conversing in another language, we are aware of greater time pressure than when speaking our first language. By the time we have worked out what we want to say, the topic of the conversation has often moved on, so that what we wanted to say is no longer relevant. This is one of the commonest problems reported to us by our students once they have started their degree courses.

One way to practise speaking English under time pressure is called 4-3-2 (Maurice 1983). The version below is our adaptation of the original suggestion.

4-3-2

1 Find a text (such as a newspaper article). Read it and make brief notes, on a separate piece of paper, of the main points. Put the article away, but keep your notes.
2 Record yourself giving an oral summary based on your notes. Allow yourself **4 minutes**.
3 Rewind and listen; monitor your performance – are there any words you need to look at again in the article? Do you need to check their pronunciation (sound and stress) in the dictionary? If so, do that.
4 Rewind. Make a second recording, but this time give yourself only **3 minutes**.
5 Repeat Step 3.
6 Make a final recording, summarising the text in **2 minutes**.

Of course, 4-3-2 is a very artificial exercise. But our students tell us it has the advantage of making you think about what is essential and getting the maximum information into the shortest time.

Practice task 3

Try out the 4-3-2 technique. When you have completed all six Steps, discuss with other students how well you think it worked for you.

Feedback

The strategies we have suggested so far have focused on different forms of practice which you can work on alone. Working alone has the advantage of private practice, but the disadvantage of omitting the other main requisite for improving your spoken English – the opportunity to receive feedback.

In the language classroom you can get feedback and correction from the teacher. In the world outside, you need to adopt effective strategies for getting feedback in everyday interaction with other speakers of English.

Our last two suggestions come from students who had already completed pre-session English language classes and had found ways of using their friends and flatmates as sources of feedback.

I try to involve myself in situations where I have to speak and discuss with people – in kitchens, social events, visits to friends and so forth. Or I record myself and try to improve my pronunciation by repeating again and again the words that are difficult for me to pronounce. I also request friends to help me by pointing out my weak points in speaking.

I tried to express myself clearly by talking with someone. But in many cases I cannot make myself understood because of my wrong spoken English. Sometimes I found I had to think for a while to choose words. However if I speak more, I feel more confident.

(Anderson and Lynch 1996: 124)

Both the students realised the importance of getting feedback on their spoken English mistakes. However, this is not easy outside class. In many English-speaking countries, you will find that local people will be reluctant to correct you, even if you ask them to. It's a question of culture: explicitly correcting how someone else speaks is unusual in conversation among native speakers. It is of course perfectly natural – and even expected – for language teachers to correct your mistakes in the classroom, but that doesn't happen much in ordinary conversation. When native speakers correct each other, they usually do so indirectly, as in the example on the opposite page:

Fred:	*How did you get there?*
Barney:	*On the 41.*
Fred:	*The 41?*
Barney:	*I mean the 41A.*

The 'correction' occurs through Barney querying the correctness of what Fred has said, which leads Fred to correct himself (*'I mean...'*). In English social conversation, a person risks being considered impolite and arrogant if they directly correct someone else. For these reasons, many people will feel uncomfortable about correcting your English.

So this is a real problem for language learners. You want feedback in order to make faster progress, but how can you get it if you don't have access to an English teacher to correct you? Here are two strategies which you can apply in everyday conversation.

Observe others' reactions

Don't ask other people to correct you, because that may have no effect. Instead, carefully observe the reactions of people you talk to as you are speaking. They will probably give little signals when you have said something they don't understand – such as frowning, giving you a blank look, or leaning towards you to hear better. Try to work out what it was that caused the problem. Rephrase it and make a note to practise it in your audio diary.

Check what others thought you said

One way that native speakers do provide feedback when they have had difficulty understanding you is when they tell you what they thought you said – for example, *'Oh ORANGE – I thought you said A RANGE.'* This is really useful, because it gives you a clear idea of what it was that caused their problem. In other words, it tells you what your English sounds like to others. So when you're in a conversation and have said something that other people haven't understood, ask the person to tell you what it was they thought you said. We think you will often find that it was syllable-stress within a word that was the problem.

Practice task 4

Think up a one-sentence statement, of around 10–12 words, about your home city or town. Don't include any numbers or statistics. Don't write it down; keep it in your head.

Work with other students (in a group or as a whole class) and take it in turns to make your statement. You can say it ONLY ONCE. The other students write down what they think you said. When everyone has had their turn as speaker, compare what speakers said and listeners heard. Be prepared for some shocks!

A final point: intercultural communication in spoken English

We have focused on interaction with native speakers. However, we want to highlight two reasons why it is helpful to practise speaking with other international students as well. First, there is a demographic reason: in many university situations around the world you are more likely to find yourself in a mixed group of native and non-native speakers of English, or a group where everyone is an international student. In that sense, universities reflect the global role of English, which is now used for daily communication by more non-native speakers than native speakers.

The second reason for encouraging you to get plenty of practice in speaking to other international students is that it can be more useful to practise your spoken English with them than with native speakers. Here is how a Greek student put it.

I think it's good practice to listen to other foreign speakers talking about your field. You have to get used to their accents, in the same way as you have get used to British people's different accents. In fact, there are bigger differences between British accents than between foreigners, I think. So it's all good practice and helps to find out more about the subject.

(Anderson and Lynch 1996: 22)

Speaking with other international students can help to build your confidence in listening and the fluency in speaking that you need to participate effectively in your academic studies. Regular, active practice and efficient use of feedback provide the best combination for effective improvement in your spoken English beyond the language classroom.

Discussion task 3

We have discussed some of the strategies our students have recommended, on the basis of their experience in an English-speaking country. Can you suggest other ways of getting practice and feedback after the course?

Teacher's guide

Scenarios

BACKGROUND NOTES

Objectives

The scenarios making up Part 1 of the course are based on the work of Robert Di Pietro (1987), who developed a particular type of role-play in which language learners are presented with a situation where they have to resolve or cope with a potential conflict. For example, in the fourth scenario in *Study Speaking*, a student has to ask a tutor to extend the deadline for her essay – a situation which is probably familiar to most of us (from one side or the other!) but which is much more difficult to manage in a foreign language. The key to a successful performance in a scenario is a combination of skills of persuasion and compromise, plus flexibility under pressure. All the scenarios featured in the book are based on actual experiences of our past EAP students.

Structure

Each scenario involves three main stages. In the first, **rehearsal**, the learners are assigned to one of two role groups (Role A or B), which separately discuss possible routes to their goal. In the second, **performance**, pairs of students from each role-group play out the scenario, keeping as closely as possible to the overall strategy that their group has planned. The final stage, **debriefing**, gives the class the chance to assess how well they have done, to suggest possible improvements or alternatives, and to focus on language form.

Since the first edition of *Study Speaking* we have experimented with different forms and sequences of performance, and the one we mention first is the one we have found works best. After describing that procedure, we briefly summarise some of the alternatives.

Procedure

Stage 1: Rehearsal

Divide the class in half; one group reads the text for Role A (always the 'student' role) and the other reads the text for Role B (the office-holder or member of staff). Ask the students to study their text carefully, and to discuss any questions about the information or the language in their role text.

The practical maximum number in these groups is about eight students. If you have more than 16 people in the class, it is better to divide them into four groups, so that two A groups and two B groups can run in parallel. Rehearsal works best when the students in a group sit close together. This contributes to a feeling of unity and cooperation; it also has the practical advantage that their discussion can be kept secret from their 'opponents' in the other role-group.

The main aim of the rehearsal is for the groups to take in the background information for their scenario role, to establish their goal and to plan their strategy. Rehearsal also enables the group members to pool ideas and suggestions, reduces anxiety about the coming performance and allows them to learn new language from each other.

The A and B role instructions are quite detailed in some cases, and you need to allow plenty of time for the students to study their texts. If you find the instructions too restrictive – or inappropriate to your local teaching context – then you can of course adapt them by replacing or deleting specific parts of the role instructions. When a group asks for assistance at the planning stage, we suggest you provide the help they want, but try to avoid either imposing your own ideas on them or giving mini-lectures. The students should get used to relying on each other for ideas about strategy, which will help them to make effective use of the planning time in later scenarios.

You will find some suggestions for useful vocabulary in the *Teaching notes*, starting on page 146. However, we don't usually teach the vocabulary in advance, unless a group makes a specific request to which it would be an appropriate response. We think it is better to allow learners to identify a language need for themselves, rather than the teacher *assuming* that they have gaps in their (L2) knowledge.

Stage 2: Performance
It's important not to think of this as a theatrical 'performance'. The two students in each pair are *players*, rather than actors; they are trying to achieve the goals established by their group, not enacting a script written in advance. Flexibility in coping with the unexpected from the opponent is a key element.

Suggested procedure
The way we now use the scenarios in class is as follows:
1 When the A and B groups have completed their preparation, get them to form up in A+B pairs with someone from the other group. The pairs should sit as far away from other pairs as is practical.
2 All the pairs then play the scenario 'privately', simultaneously, so that everyone in the class is working in parallel. If you have an

odd number of students, you should partner the one remaining student. If you have an even number, you can monitor and take notes on different pairs' performance.

3 When all the pairs have finished, ask them to return to their original places. Call for two volunteers (A and B) to play the scenario again, for the rest of the class. We prefer to ask two players who have not just been working together, because that increases the element of surprise; but it may help less confident students to perform again with their opponent from the previous stage.

4 The two players need to be in a position where they can be seen and heard easily. We sit them facing each other across a table. You need to record the performance in some way: pen-and-paper notes, on audiocassette or – ideally – on videocassette. Logistically, the simplest method is to take notes; it has the advantage of giving you an 'edited' selective version, which is ready for immediate use. Audio- or video-recording gives you a more objective version of the players' performance, but makes it more difficult to locate and replay the sequences you wish to comment on.

5 The next step – a second public performance – depends on the size of your class. If you divided a large class into four groups, then you should now ask two players from the other A and B groups to perform. If your class consists of only two groups, ask two new A and B players to do the scenario. Try to ensure that there is enough time for a second performance, but sometimes you may find there simply isn't. If so, go straight on to the debriefing.

Stage 3: Debriefing

Robert Di Pietro emphasised the need for the language learners to take an active part in the evaluation of the performances, and the importance of getting the learners to analyse both the content (strategy) and form (language) of the performance. So his term *debriefing* is not just another way of saying 'correction by the teacher'; it should be a genuinely *collaborative* discussion of what was done and said in a performance.

After the public performance, begin by asking the students for their general reaction to what they have seen. We suggest you work from content (strategy) and information through to language, so that the debriefing leads to the airing of general points about the best way to persuade someone to take your view, and not just the correction of individual language errors.

STRATEGY	*Did they manage to get what they wanted?*
	Did one player come away the loser?
INFORMATION	*Did they use relevant role information provided?*
	Did they forget or change any details?
COMMUNICATION	*Were there any breakdowns in communication?*
	How (and how well) did they resolve them?
LANGUAGE	*Did their performance reveal any significant gaps in grammar, vocabulary or pronunciation?*

The first two issues are about the *content* of the performances. First, what about the strategies adopted by the two players? Was the outcome what they had planned when they were preparing for the scenario? Do they feel that there was a 'winner', or was the result a compromise between players A and B? Secondly, how well did they use the information they were given in their role instructions?

The third and fourth issues are about *form*, the language used by the players. Were there parts of the performance where communication between the players got stuck or even broke down? If so, can they identify the source of the difficulty? Did they notice any items of vocabulary or grammar that they would like to comment on themselves, or to have your comments on? For example, we once recorded a Scenario 3 in class, in which the Student and the Accommodation Officer talked at cross-purposes for 10 minutes or so: the Student had asked whether she could *live in* a particular flat while it was being renovated, but the Accommodation Officer understood he was being asked whether she could *leave* her things in the flat during the renovation.

As far as possible, encourage the students to raise queries and points themselves rather than take the lead yourself in listing the errors you noted during the performance. We find that students' questions are often on the lines of '*Our player said (X). Is there a better way of saying that?*' At this point, you may find it useful to refer to expressions provided in the *Teaching notes* (pages 146–150).

Alternative procedures

As we mentioned earlier, we have tried out variations on the *Performance* and *Debriefing* stages, which we will summarise here. You may be able to adopt or adapt them to suit your teaching situation.

Stage 2: Performance
Omitting the parallel pair work
If you are working in a context where for some reason it is not possible to have all the students working simultaneously in 'parallel pairs', then skip Stages 1 and 2 of the suggested *Performance sequence*. Ask a pair of volunteers to do a public performance as soon as the A and B groups have completed their preparation.

Bringing in an assistant (or second teacher)
On our pre-sessional course at Edinburgh we have a non-teacher course assistant who participates in speaking classes. The assistant works with one of the groups at the Preparation stage, while the teacher works with the other. This means that the students are able to check points with a native speaker informant throughout the Preparation stage. The assistant is then available as a partner during the parallel pair work when we have an odd number of students. Sometimes we also ask the assistant to play one of the roles in a public performance, if the students are reluctant to volunteer – which tends to happen at the start of a course, before they know each other well. (For further details of the role and value of the course assistant, see Lynch and Anderson 2003.)

Rotating pairs
This activity can be used when you have pairs working simultaneously on the scenario, whether or not you are recording them. It works well either at the Performance stage, or after Debriefing – or transcribing. When the student A+B pairs have completed a scenario, you ask all the A players to move clockwise to the next B player, so that the new pairs can repeat the scenario. (In fact, 'repeat' is not quite the right term, because the arrival of a new partner means that the second scenario is never a word-for-word duplication of the first.)

Debriefing using recorded performances
Using a single pair's performance: Proof-listening
A recording of a pair's scenario performance is potentially valuable material for peer feedback as well as teacher feedback. However, some teachers are worried that getting students to comment on others' performances will lead to confrontation rather than collaboration. To reduce that risk, we have developed a form of debriefing that we call *proof-listening*, by analogy with *proof-reading*. It consist of three cycles, each of which gives different people the primary right to speak.

Cycle 1

During Cycle 1, only the *players* featured in the recording have the right to speak. As their performance is replayed, they tell you to stop the tape at any point where they realise they made a mistake, or where what they said was not quite what they wanted to say. In this way, they can 'edit' the slips in their performance, and get advice from the teacher (and other students) on a better way of expressing their meaning. Then rewind the tape.

Cycle 2

In the second cycle, you replay the tape and this time you ask the *other students* to tell you to stop it when they want to ask the players for repetition or clarification, or to query a point of grammar, word-choice or pronunciation. You may find they also ask about possible differences between a word that a speaker has used and one they themselves used when they did the task.

Cycle 3

This is where the *teacher* takes the lead. If you have taken notes on additional points for comment, you may not need to replay the tape a third time. Draw the students' attention to anything you think they should have noticed during the first two cycles. This cycle is particularly important if you are teaching students *with the same first language*, because they tend to make the same mistakes and so may not identify them in others' performances. For this reason, you may find that Cycle 2 is relatively short, and Cycle 3 rather longer. Conversely, with multilingual classes, Cycle 2 tends to take longer – because the listeners detect more points to ask about in the two players' English – and the third cycle is shorter.

The main point of proof-listening is to encourage noticing, and in a way that gives the two players – the people most at risk of losing face – the opportunity to edit and improve their performance before their peers comment in the second cycle.

Using multiple recordings of parallel pair work

If you have been able to set up the parallel pair work, then it is worth considering ways of recording and using all the pairs' performances. On our pre-sessional programme at Edinburgh we hold the Performance stage of the scenario in a large study room, equipped with audiocassette recorders set up in pairs at strategic intervals around the edge of the room. The pairs of recorders are far enough from the neighbouring pairs to allow students to record their conversation on their own cassettes without interference from other pairs.

The fact that every student in a class can record themselves on their own cassette allows us to exploit the recordings for individual post-task 'noticing'. The activity we have found most useful involves getting the students to transcribe and edit their original recording – a more detailed form of 'noticing' than is practised in proof-listening.

Transcribing

In transcribing, the following rules apply.

1 Each pair chooses a section of their recording lasting about <u>2 minutes</u>. It should be a section where the two partners spoke a roughly equal amount of English.

2 They listen to their own recording through headphones, on separate cassette players, transcribing their conversation verbatim (exactly), including repetitions and changes of mind.

3 They compare their two handwritten transcripts and sort out any differences in what was said. In cases of dispute, assume the speaker is right!

4 They use a word processor and save their agreed transcript, then print out three copies (one for each of them and one for the teacher). This is *Transcript 1*.

5 They copy Transcript 1 to a new file, and then together make corrections and improvements <u>on screen</u>. They save the corrected and edited version as *Transcript 2*. Again they print three copies.

6 They give the teacher a paper copy of the two transcripts, and also Transcript 2 on a floppy disk.

7 The teacher takes away the materials, corrects and reformulates Transcript 2 into *Transcript 3*, and then prints it out.

8 In a later lesson, the teacher returns Transcript 3, which the students then compare with Transcript 2. They analyse the changes and discuss them with the teacher if they are in any doubt as to why a change has been made.

9 The pair of students go back to the study room and re-record their scenario twice – once using Transcript 3, and once without.

If you have doubts about how your students would take to the transcribing task, or how much trouble they would take over the very detailed work it requires, you might like to read a report on our Edinburgh students' self-transcribing (Lynch 2001a). Not only did they notice a large number of slips and errors, they enjoyed the task so much that they asked to do it again in the next course – good evidence that they perceived the task to be valuable.

When self-transcribing works well, it can develop the scenario into an extended activity over several lessons. We timetable it as two or three 90-minute sessions, depending on whether the students do the transcribing in their own time or in class. The breakdown of tasks is:

Lesson 1: Preparation and Performance (in parallel pairs)

Lesson 2: (or a home assignment): Pairs to complete Transcripts 1 and 2

Lesson 3: (or the second lesson): The teacher to discuss each pair's Transcript 3 with them; the pairs to re-record the scenario, then give a final Performance before the Debriefing.

TEACHING NOTES

Scenario 1 LANGUAGE CENTRE

See the *Background notes* section (pages 139–146) for the alternative options for Scenarios. The basic procedure occupies 90 minutes, or two 45-minute lessons as shown below.

Preparation: 15 min

Performance: 30 min (parallel pairs 10 min; public performance by one or two pairs 5–10 min each)

Debriefing: 20–25 min (for example, proof-listening)

Follow-up performance: 20 min (in rotating pairs)

If you have recording facilities and more time at your disposal, you can get the students to transcribe their performances, as set out on pages 145–146.

For each scenario we list some expressions that our students have found they needed. We normally provide them at the Debriefing stage, but with weaker groups it may be necessary to give them during Preparation.

Student

I'm sorry to bother you, but I wanted to ask about...
I'm a bit worried about...
Everyone else on my course is a native speaker, so....
I really don't feel that my... is good enough.
After all I only got just over 60.
Why can't I have a place?

Language course director

The problem is that...
Have you any reason to think you have serious language problems?
Instead of coming to classes, why not...?
I think you should...
We have to give priority to...

Scenario 2 LIBRARY

With this scenario, it's a good idea to check that the students who are preparing the Librarian role realise that it was *their* decision to restrict the opening hours and not to allow students to borrow books, and not a general university rule. That gives the Librarians the option – though they are not always willing to use it – of making an exception for the Student and allowing him to borrow, assuming that it doesn't lead to many more 'me-toos' making the same request.

Here are some of the expressions we have elicited from students or provided ourselves.

Student

I was wondering whether I could...
Can I explain my problem?
I can see you're busy but...
I'm afraid that would be too late for me to...
Is there a rule that says I can't borrow?

Librarian

I appreciate your problem, but...
If I make one exception, then I will have to...
Couldn't you...?
How about...?
Well, perhaps I can lend you one book overnight.

Scenario 3 FINDING ACCOMMODATION

The blank rent 'boxes' in the role materials should be completed with whatever you and the class think is a realistic rent in the appropriate currency.

For the task dynamics to work best, the figure in the Student's information should be roughly midway between the two rents in the Accommodation Officer's information. For example, current figures suitable for Edinburgh would be £500 for the Student's budget, and £480 and £530 respectively for the two blank boxes in the Accommodation Officer's information. This means that the Students have to weigh up the advantages of the two flats – one available now with the higher but inclusive rent, against the cheaper one that will mean several weeks' wait.

Useful language
Student

I hope I'm not being a nuisance...
I really do need to find a flat nearer to...

How soon would I be able to move in?
That's more than I can afford.

Accommodation officer

Well, you have to realise that…
I'm afraid there's not really very much more I can do for you.
I could give you a list of agencies.

Scenario 4 DEADLINE FOR AN ESSAY

There are two sample performances of this scenario on side B of the cassette. The transcripts are shown on pages 212–220. One was recorded by two native speakers – a Scottish male as the Student and an English female as the Tutor. The other sample was recorded by two international postgraduate students at the University of Edinburgh – a Chinese female Tutor and a Portuguese male Student.

There are various ways of using the sample performances.

- You could play them to your class at the first Scenario session, before doing any of the scenarios, to show how the activity works.
- You could play them before or after the class has done Scenario 4.
- You could get the students to compare their performance with either the native or non-native sample.
- You could (also) get the students to listen to the two samples and compare the different tactics used by the speakers.
- We tend to use the sample performances as part of the Feedback stage, after discussing our students' own performances.

We've found that some EAP students prefer to listen to the non-native sample, because they think the native speaker version is too far beyond their capabilities, and represents an unachievable target. If the group feels that way, we use the international students' version.

Useful language

Student

Is there any chance of getting an extension for this essay?
I realise that it would be inconvenient, but…
I know I have already had an extension but…
I really did everything I could to get hold of the book but…

Tutor

This isn't the first time you've…
But it's a question of fairness.
I have to think about the other students.
You should have had plenty of time to…
Why didn't you come to tell me about this earlier?

Scenario 5 EXAMINATION RESULTS
Useful language
Student

> *I had a feeling it wouldn't be very good.*
> *I think there are probably a number of reasons why I didn't do very well.*
> *I've probably spent too much time on...*
> *I realise I'm going to have to...*

Director of Studies

> *I'm afraid your result wasn't too good.*
> *You seem to be having some problems with...*
> *To be honest, we're worried about your work.*
> *There's a real risk that you...*
> *We feel that you should go to the English language classes.*

Scenario 6 CHANGING ACCOMMODATION
Useful language
Student

> *I can't stay in the room.*
> *It's having a bad effect on my work.*
> *I need a quieter place to study.*
> *Isn't there another room available?*
> *Can I move to a different residence?*

Accommodation Manager

> *I do sympathise but...*
> *There's nothing available at the moment.*
> *You might be able to move in the vacation.*
> *That's not really my responsibility.*

Scenario 7 PROJECT RESULTS

This scenario was designed with postgraduate students in mind, so you may need to adapt the details if you are teaching undergraduate or pre-university students. It is intended to lead to discussion – and explanation by the teacher – of the role of External Examiners, which most students (local as well as international) are unfamiliar with.

In Britain, the External Examiner plays an active part in taking an overview of students' work on a degree course, and individual students who feel their work has been harshly marked can ask the course director to ask the External Examiner to look at their work.

We have deliberately included two words (*rambling* and *messy*) which are likely to be unfamiliar to students. For obvious reasons, you should not explain them; their meanings are available in the Course Director's role instructions, so he can explain them to the Student during the performance. In our experience, markers often use informal comments that are not clear to international students (such as 'fuzzy', 'long-winded', 'needs to be snappier') and this task was designed to alert them to the need to clarify precisely what feedback means.

Useful language
Student

> I don't understand some of the written feedback.
> But I showed the project to a tutor and he said it was all right.
> My project is as good as other students'.
> Could you read it yourself and see whether you agree with the mark?

Course Director

> But both markers thought it was a low Pass.
> No, that's not how the marking process works.
> I really don't have much time at the moment.
> That's why we have an External Examiner.
> I can ask the External Examiner to read the project and check the mark.
> Well, not for the moment. We do it at the end of the taught part of the course.

Scenario 8 RESEARCH PROPOSAL
Useful language
Student

> I don't think the committee has been very fair with me.
> There are several things that I think you ought to know.
> If I had had more contact with my supervisor...I would have...
> He's often unavailable.
> He's usually too busy to see me.
> This is very serious for me personally.
> I can't afford to wait six months.

Head of Department

> I do sympathise but...
> The committee's decision was unanimous.
> Your proposal just isn't strong enough.
> I'm afraid we can't change the decision because of your funding.
> That's not something we can take into account.
> But you don't have to wait six months.
> Six months is just a deadline. You can resubmit the proposal before then.

Discussion skills

BACKGROUND NOTES

Objectives

The aim of the *Discussion skills* work is to give students practice in the type of interaction that they will meet in small-group discussions at college or university, such as tutorials or seminars. The intention is that these materials should be used flexibly. You can select, resequence or adapt the tasks to suit your students' interests and skill level, and the available lesson time in your programme. When you plan lessons around these *Discussion skills* materials, our advice is to maximise the lesson time students spend *discussing*, and to make sure there is enough time for *feedback* on their performance.

In each unit, we focus on a common language function, or *speech act*, which students are likely to need to express in group discussions; for example, explaining, disagreeing or asking for clarification. There is a brief presentation of *Useful language* items which could be appropriately used to express that function. We have also designed the *Discussion points* so that students are occasionally prompted to express the unit's highlighted function (such as *'explain…'*, *'give your opinion about…'*).

However, our overriding aim is to provide opportunities for natural interaction – focusing on the effective communication of ideas – rather than to practise particular items of language. In designing the discussion tasks, we have not attempted in any way to restrict the language that students use to those functions highlighted in the unit, or covered earlier. Students are likely to express any number of the communicative functions we have selected, as well as others we do not deal with, in every discussion task. The list of functions, together with the selection of *Useful language* items, is intended not as an underlying syllabus of 'bits' of English to be accumulated, but as a regular opportunity for students to focus their attention on particular sets of linguistic forms that we assume they may find it useful to deploy.

We have tried to select topics and frame questions so that they will work equally well with mixed nationality, multilingual groups and with single-nationality, monolingual groups. But we encourage you to adapt tasks wherever you can to make them more relevant to your students' situation and interests.

Unit contents

There is enough material in the *Discussion skills* section of each unit for 90 minutes of class time. Each unit contains:

- a list of 'Useful language' associated with the functional focus of the unit, and one or two Practice exercises
- two Discussion points, comprising Preparation and Discussion activities, which focus on issues related to the unit topic (see *Course map*).

In most units, one of the Discussion points is based on one, or several, short reading texts, which students should be asked to read <u>in advance</u> of the session. The *Teaching notes* that follow these Background notes offer brief guidance on each unit and an Additional discussion point, which can be used as supplementary material, if required.

Timing

Below are suggested timings for a 90-minute *Discussion skills* lesson. Groups will vary in the amount of time they will need or want to spend on each activity, so we have estimated minimum timings for each phase. (Note: In our experience, groups with more advanced language skills often take *more* time to complete discussion tasks than lower-level groups, because they are better able to sustain the discussion.)

	Activity timing (minutes)	Running total (minutes)
Useful language & Practice	10–15	10–15
Set up groups for Discussion point, check instructions are clear	5	15–20
Discussion point 1	15–20	30–40
Feedback	5–10	35–50
Discussion point 2	15–20	50–70
Feedback	10	60–90

A faster group following the <u>minimum</u> timings suggested would have time for the Additional discussion point in the *Teaching notes*.

Suggested procedure
Before the lesson

Set the input text, or other material – see the unit's *Teaching notes* – to be read as preparation for the Discussion skills session. Reading the texts in class would take up time that should be spent in discussion.

In the lesson

1 Useful language.
2 Practice.
3 Divide the class into groups, for Discussion.
4 If the Discussion is based on a text they have read in advance, check whether the students have had any problems understanding the material.
5 Check the instructions are clear, and tell the students to begin. (There may be an individual Preparation task before the Discussion.)
6 Monitor the Discussion.
7 Make sure there is enough time – at least 10 minutes – to provide feedback (stop the discussion if necessary).
8 Give feedback.
9 Repeat 4–8.

Grouping

The size of the groups for Discussion points can vary; but with less-fluent English speakers we suggest starting with groups of three or four, as less-confident students are likely to find it difficult to contribute in larger groups. Group size could be increased to six or eight later in the course, as confidence grows, to reflect more accurately what will happen in tutorials and seminars in many universities and colleges. If you think there is a risk that a minority of confident individuals will dominate the discussion, you could group those students together.

Monitoring

It is important to monitor the groups' interaction, not just so as to be able to comment on faults or weaknesses, but also to make a note of examples of effective language use. Spend a few minutes at a time listening in to each group and making notes of language or interaction points for feedback. Respond to any requests for language help (*How do you say…?*), but avoid intervening to sort out communication problems, unless they seriously hold up the discussion.

It is important to allow and encourage students to develop effective strategies for dealing with communication breakdowns themselves, as those strategies will be necessary when they use English beyond the classroom. Make a note of what went wrong, and whether or not it was successfully repaired and how, for feedback.

Feedback

Try to stop the Discussion soon enough to allow time for feedback; we would suggest 10 minutes as a minimum. Comment on both *interaction* and *language* issues.

Interaction

One useful area to highlight is any communication breakdowns: what caused them, and how successfully (or otherwise) they were repaired. In addition to any you observed in monitoring, ask the students to recall any cases where there were communication difficulties. Common interaction faults include the following:

- Speaker
  - repeating over and over again a word that has not been understood
  - not checking whether the listener has understood
- Listener
  - not making clear that they haven't understood
  - not making clear <u>what</u> they haven't understood (for example, by simply repeating the problem phrase with rising intonation)
  - not making clear that a question is a question
  - not checking that what they have understood is correct
  - not being assertive enough – that is, not persisting with a question.

Language

Going through a miscellaneous assortment of language points may seem arbitrary and confusing to students. Focusing only, or mainly, on how well the students expressed the language function highlighted in the unit provides a coherent basis for selecting points.

In commenting on vocabulary and grammar, it is important to consider not only <u>correctness</u> but also <u>appropriacy</u> of expression and <u>collocation</u>. Pronunciation may cause problems, of course. Here we would advise focusing mainly on <u>stress</u>. Although students should be aware of which specific phonemes cause their listeners most comprehension problems – and some remedial practice may be appropriate with monolingual groups – the source of real-life misunderstandings of non-native learners' English is often incorrect stress placement, either within a single word or on part of a sentence.

Alternative procedure

Working through a set of *Discussion skills* material in the printed sequence, beginning with the *Useful language* work, provides class-work of the conventional PPP type (Presentation, Practice, Production). An alternative approach, more in keeping with the principles of task-based learning, is to start with one or both of the Discussion points, without pre-teaching any specific language. Then, when monitoring the groups' performance in discussion, you identify areas of their language use which could be improved, and select material for follow-up form-focused work, perhaps in a later session. The *Useful language* section in the unit would then be one possible source of appropriate material.

Speaking logs

If you have facilities that allow students to record themselves on their own cassette during Discussion tasks, then you may also be able to get them to 'notice' and ask about aspects of their spoken English using what we call a Speaking Log. The Log is intended to encourage learners' selective attention in the process of *noticing* as they listen to recordings of their spoken English. Below is a schematic version of the Log, showing the three column headings that appear at the top of an A4 sheet of paper (in landscape mode).

Slips (mistakes and your corrections)	Queries (points you are not sure about when you listen again)	Responses (for the teacher to complete)

The students listen to themselves and focus on points they want to correct (which they each note in their *Slips* column) and words or expressions they are now unsure about (which they note under *Queries*). They then hand their Log in to the teacher, who takes it away and completes the third column by answering the student's queries. The teacher brings back the completed Logs for the owners to read and discuss.

If your facilities don't allow students to make individual recordings, the Log can also be used by pairs or groups working collaboratively on a group recording.

Debates and role-plays

One way in which the Discussions in Part 2 differ from the Scenario performances in Part 1 is that in the Discussions the students express their own real opinions, speaking as themselves, rather than views and attitudes that are largely determined by the roles assigned to them. Having to make up their own minds about the issues in question, and articulate, defend and perhaps modify those views in discussion, simulates more closely the experience that students will encounter in university tutorials and seminars. This should be particularly valuable preparation for students who have not previously been required – or perhaps allowed – to give their own opinions on the content of their studies. Such students often have particular difficulty adjusting to an academic environment in which they are expected to participate in critical debate.

However, we recognise that some, often more confident, students enjoy the element of theatricality in more artificial discussion formats – such as role-plays and formal debates – which require individual participants to adopt standpoints that do not necessarily reflect their real attitudes and opinions. While such activities have disadvantages as EAP tasks – they are less authentic than free discussion in their relationship to what most students will need to do in their university studies, and formal debates, in particular, distribute participation very unequally – debates and role-plays do have the benefit that they oblige students to look critically at issues from perspectives they may not otherwise consider.

In the *Teaching notes*, we have therefore identified some Discussion points that lend themselves to alternative treatment either as debates (in Units 2, 6 and 8) or a role-play (Unit 5). The *Teaching notes* for Unit 2 contain some comments on organising formal debates. Suggested role specifications are given in the *Teaching notes* for Unit 5.

TEACHING NOTES
Unit 1 Work
Giving your opinion

TO BE READ IN ADVANCE
The text for Discussion point 2 (Preparation 1) is intended to prompt reflection on the topic. If possible, ask the students to read it in advance of the lesson. However, if this material is to be used as the first lesson in a course, and it is not possible to set homework in advance, you can omit the reading and go straight to Preparation 2.

Additional discussion points

Below are two suggestions for further discussion topics on the theme of work.

1　Do you know this word?

　　teleworking [/ˈteliwɜːkɪŋ/ UK (US **telecommuting**)] *noun* [U] working at home, while communicating with your office by computer and telephone.　　　　　*Cambridge Learner's Dictionary*

In some countries, teleworking is becoming very common. Is it common in your country? Would you prefer to work in this way? Discuss the reasons for your answers. Has anyone in your group had experience of this?

2　In many countries the population is ageing rapidly. The world median age is expected to rise from 26.5 years in 2000 to 36.2 in 2050. How is this likely to affect work?[1]

Unit 2 Food
Agreeing and disagreeing

> TO BE READ IN ADVANCE
> We suggest that you allocate the reading texts for Discussion point 2 (Preparation 2) in advance, to be prepared before the Discussion session. (See below for details.)

An alternative way of introducing the materials would be to ask the students to discuss (in groups or plenary) the following question.

> Do you agree with the statement: *It is easier to agree than disagree in discussions*? Explain your answer.

Useful language

The point to stress here is that expressing disagreement does not require elaborately polite formulae. Depending on the background and experience of your class, it may be helpful to point out that disagreeing is expected in discussion at all levels of anglophone academic culture, and is unlikely to cause offence unless it is angry or personal.

Discussion point 2

Preparation 2

It will save lesson time if you set these texts to be read in advance. There are six texts altogether; their lengths vary, though none are

---

[1] UN Population Division. *World Population Prospects: The 2000 Revision.* New York: United Nations, 2000.

very long. Texts 1, 3 and 4 are pro-GM; 2, 5 and 6 highlight anti-GM arguments. You could ask each student in a group of six to read and prepare to summarise one text, allocating the shorter texts, 2 and 6, to weaker students. With smaller groups you could set stronger students two texts.

With weaker groups, we suggest setting one text per student. As less confident students may tend to say little in larger groups, we suggest limiting the group size to a maximum of four, and selecting just four of the texts for use in this task, for example 2, 3, 4 and 6 (this provides a balance of pro- and anti- arguments, and focuses on two aspects: the safety of GM food, and its capacity to feed the world's growing population).

Additional discussion point

If you need more group discussion material, you could use the questions below. The topic would also be suitable for Unit 4 (Health).

- Do you consider your personal eating habits to be 'healthy'? Explain your answer.
- Do you avoid eating any types of food for reasons of health or for any other reason apart from your personal tastes?
- Is the typical diet in your country (or region) healthy, or do people tend to eat too little or too much of certain types of food? Are any common illnesses or other problems in your country related to dietary factors?
- Have the eating habits of people in your country changed in recent years? If so, in what ways? Why have these changes occurred? What effects – if any – do you think these changes are having, or will have in the future, on the nation's health? Are there likely to be any other consequences – for example, cultural, economic or political?

This topic would be suitable for a Debate (see note below). Traditionally, debating motions are expressed as statements rather than questions – a suitable wording might be 'GM technology is necessary and beneficial'.

Notes on debates

Debating societies thrive in schools and universities in many parts of the world, and many students will be familiar with the idea of formal debating. Debates are chaired discussions which follow a conventional format involving a sequence of short prepared or extemporised speeches arguing for and against a controversial proposition ('the motion'), an opportunity for contributions from the audience ('the floor'), and then a vote.

The usual format is for a number of speakers – usually two or three for each side – to take turns to propose or oppose the motion. Comments are invited 'from the floor', and then a speaker from each side sums up, restating their side's arguments and rebutting those of the other side. Finally, the audience vote on the motion, which is either carried or defeated. Strict rules govern the length and type of contribution at each stage of the debate; a very concise and down-to-earth account of their version of the rules is given on the web site of University College London's Debating Society: www.ucl-debating.org.uk/pages/rules.htm.

Once the students are confident about the rules you are using, ask a student to take on the role of chairperson (rehearse some formal chairing language with them, such as 'I now call on X to oppose the motion').

If time, numbers, your students' confidence or interests do not favour a full-blown formal debate, you could simplify the format. For example, one or two students could be chosen to prepare short – say, 2-minute – speeches for each side (if two, they need to work as a team and agree on the arguments each will use). Then there could be time for questions to the speakers and open, informal discussion by the whole group. Optionally, one speaker for each side sums up (and rebuts), and a vote is taken. If you have a very large class, you could divide it into smaller groups of, say, eight to ten, and have several simultaneous debates, to give more people the opportunity to give speeches and to create a less daunting audience.

Unit 3 Language
Explaining

> TO BE READ IN ADVANCE
> There is no reading text for this Unit, but students will need time to think about their individual responses to the Discussion points. We suggest that you set up the discussion groups and allocate Discussion point 2 topics before the session, and ask the students to do the individual Preparation tasks for Discussion points 1 and 2 as preparatory homework.

Useful language
The language presented here is relatively informal. Some students may suggest more formal expressions such as …*is a factor in*… or *consequently*, which would be appropriate in academic writing, but could sound rather stilted in natural speech.

Expressing certainty/uncertainty

Our answers to the questions are:

I think 4
It's likely that 6
I'm certain 1/2
I'd say 5
It could be that 8
It could well be that 7
Possibly 9
I'm sure 3 (this is used more casually than 'I'm certain')
There's no doubt 1

The *Practice* exercise on expressing certainty/uncertainty should be kept very brief; it is not intended to prompt extended discussion, but simply to practise manipulating the forms. Students make their own selection of topics.

Discussion points 1 and 2

The discussion tasks in this Unit have a secondary 'learner-training' agenda, being designed to raise students' awareness of aspects of the language learning process, and get them to reflect on their own learning strategies. We hope this will make a useful contribution to students' development as learners of English.

If the available time permits only one discussion point, *Discussion point 2* has the potential practical benefit to the students of increasing their awareness of the range of strategic options open to them.

Additional discussion point

If you need further discussion material, this Additional Discussion point develops one of the issues raised in *Discussion point 1* (but could be done even if *Discussion point 1* were omitted).

Preparation

Here again is the first statement in *Discussion point 1*.

It is easier for children than for adults to learn English as a non-native language.

1 Do you agree? Why (not)?
2 If you haven't discussed this already, find out what the others in your group think.
3 Read the following text. Does the writer express the same opinion as you did?

Some people think that the best time to begin studying a foreign language is in childhood, and that the younger you are, the easier it is to learn another language. There is little evidence, however, that children in language classrooms learn foreign languages any better than adults (people over the age of 15) in similar classroom situations. In fact, adults have many advantages over children: better memories, more efficient ways of organising information, longer attention spans, better study habits, and greater ability to handle complex mental tasks. Adults are often better motivated than children: they see learning a foreign language as necessary for education or career. In addition, adults are particularly sensitive to correctness of grammar and appropriateness of vocabulary, two factors that receive attention in most language classrooms.

Rubin, Joan, and Irene Thompson. *How to be a Successful Language Learner*.
Boston: Heinle and Heinle, 1982: 4.

Discuss the following questions in your group.
1 Were you surprised by what you read?
2 How persuasive did you find the arguments? Have you changed your mind? Explain your answer to the others in the group.

Unit 4 Health
Making suggestions

TO BE READ IN ADVANCE
We suggest that you ask the students to read the text on obesity for Discussion point 2 (and the task instructions) before the lesson.

The first part of the reading text for Discussion point 1 (page 63) could also be set in advance. However, part of the Preparation phase involves predicting the content of the second part of the WHO text; so if this is to be done, the students should not read the second part (top of page 64) beforehand.

Useful language
Our answers to the questions are:
  suggestion: *could*
  advice: *should, ought to* (but note that 'should' is often used in formal, official instructions to mean obligation: 'Students should ensure they arrive at the examination room in good time' is not just friendly advice!)
  necessity: *need to, have to, must.*

Had better is often used inappropriately by non-native speakers, who often intend simply to make a suggestion. In fact it implies 'necessity', and sometimes has the force of a warning: 'if you don't do it, you will find yourself in trouble', as in 'You'd better not be late!'

formal

I propose (that)…	ADVICE
I would suggest (that)…	SUGGESTION
My advice would be to…	ADVICE
I think the most effective strategy/course/ procedure would be to…	ADVICE
I believe it would be advisable to…	ADVICE
I think it's essential/vital/crucial/urgent/ most important that…	NECESSITY
Should we consider…-ing?	SUGGESTION
One option would be to…	SUGGESTION

neutral

I think what we/you/they should do is…	ADVICE
What I think we/you should do is…	ADVICE
I think it would be a good/sensible idea to …	ADVICE
I think the best way forward would be to…	ADVICE
My feeling is we/you should…	ADVICE
I wonder if you/we should…?	SUGGESTION
What do you think about the idea of…-ing?	SUGGESTION
Would there be any advantage/benefit in…-ing?	SUGGESTION

informal

If you ask me, we/you should…	ADVICE
What about/How about…-ing?	SUGGESTION
Do you think there would be any mileage in…-ing?	SUGGESTION
The main/key/most important thing is to…	NECESSITY
It might be an idea to…	SUGGESTION
We/You've really got to…	NECESSITY

Discussion point 1

Obesity, one of the risk factors for richer countries, is the topic of *Discussion point 2*, so you may prefer to <u>exclude</u> this from the discussion of countermeasures at this stage.

Discussion point 2

In case your students are unfamiliar with 'brainstorming', you may need to explain that it is a way of developing ideas, in which people work in groups, quickly suggesting as many ideas as they can think of.

Additional discussion point
Preparation (individual)
What do you consider to be the three most serious health problems in your country? Make a list.

Discussion: Option A (for single-nationality groups)

1 Compare your list with others in your group. Do you all agree? Discuss your reasons for your choices.
2 You should now decide as a group on <u>one</u> health problem which you think should be the top priority for your country's health service.
3 When you have reached an agreement on that issue, discuss <u>why</u> it is such a serious problem. Is it preventable? What is currently being done to tackle it, and what more, if anything, should be done.

Discussion: Option B (for mixed or single-nationality groups)

1 Compare your list with those of the others in your group. Explain why these problems are so serious in your country, and what the consequences are. (If several students in your group are from the same country, explain one problem each.)
2 Study the following list of people who can contribute to improving a nation's health:

doctors   architects   nurses
civil engineers   supermarket managers   teachers

3 Discuss in what ways each of these groups of people can have an effect on health. Can you add any others?
4 Individually, decide on the three or four groups you believe play the most important role. Then explain your choice to the rest of your group. If others disagree, try to persuade them to accept your opinion!
5 As a group, you should agree on which three or four groups are the most influential in improving health, and rank them in order of importance.
6 When all the groups have completed their discussion, one member of each group should explain their group's choice to the class. If there's time, the class should try to agree on a 'top three' ranking.

The Discussion Skills notes on *Unit 2 Food* contain an additional discussion task on diet, which is also relevant to *Health*.

Unit 5 Environment
Interrupting

> TO BE READ IN ADVANCE
> The two texts on environmental problems for Discussion point 1 should be read in advance. The introduction and Useful language sections also involve more reading than usual, and it would save class time if students read these beforehand.

Useful language

As with 'disagreeing' (Unit 2), the point to stress is that it is unnecessary – and uncommon – to use elaborate politeness routines, such as 'Do you mind if I come in here?' It may be helpful to point out the <u>past tense</u> forms (for example, *I just <u>wanted</u> to say, If I <u>could</u> just say…*) which are frequently used to indicate politeness.

Practice

Any other topics that everyone in the group is likely to be able to talk about with minimal preparation would work just as well. We suggest groups of four to six here, as the more intimate dynamics of a smaller group may make interruption less natural. Larger groups may prove intimidating for some students. The time limit is important – stop the discussion after 5 minutes (or sooner).

Discussion point 1
Preparation 1

An alternative procedure, which would take more class time, would be to treat this as a paired 'jigsaw reading' activity. Paired students should read <u>one</u> text each, then summarise the key points to their partners, who take notes. They could then proceed with *Preparation 2* as a paired activity.

Discussion

As far as possible, try to avoid placing students from the same country, or region of the country, in the same group, to maximise the potential 'information gap'.

Discussion point 2

We suggest using small groups of three or four for the group Preparation phase, and larger groups (say, five to eight students) for the Discussion.

Role-play

This Discussion point could be done as a role-play. On the following pages are some role descriptions for groups of up to nine that you could copy and cut up as role cards. However, we encourage you to adapt or replace these roles to make them more appropriate to your students' local context and interests. If you need to have more than nine in a group, some roles could be duplicated, or you could ask the students to suggest other roles and write cards.

Chair: City Council official

You are the convener of the Transport Consultative Group on the City Council. Your responsibility is to canvass views from a cross-section of the public on the Congestion Charge proposal. You have to chair the meeting, and report to the Council. If possible, you should try to make a recommendation to adopt, reject or modify the proposal. The Council leaders are generally in favour of introducing the charge, so if you recommend rejecting the proposal, you should have very strong reasons and an alternative proposal for reducing traffic congestion. However, if the participants cannot reach any kind of consensus, you will simply have to report the range of views expressed. You should try to be impartial and open-minded. Keep order in the meeting, and make sure everyone gets the chance to express their views. Listen carefully to the opinions expressed, question the participants, and feel free to challenge participants and make your own suggestions. As Chair, begin by explaining the purpose of the meeting.

Commuter 1

You live in the suburbs and have to travel in to work in the city centre. There is no train connection to your neighbourhood, and you have to travel by road. You go to work by bus, but the service is unreliable and very slow because of the traffic congestion in the rush hour, and this often makes you late for work. You have a car, but you don't use it for work because driving in the traffic is so unpleasant and parking is difficult and expensive. WHAT DO YOU THINK THE COUNCIL SHOULD DO?

Commuter 2

You are a partner in a very small firm of IT consultants. You live in a suburb of the city, and drive to your office in town. The journey is very slow and frustrating because of the traffic congestion, and causes you considerable stress. However, although there is a bus service and a rail link to your neighbourhood, you don't use public transport because you use your car to visit clients. The proposed charge will add greatly to your costs, and you may go out of business. You can't easily move elsewhere as most of your clients are local. WHAT ARE YOUR SUGGESTIONS FOR ALLEVIATING CONGESTION?

Factory manager

You are the local manager of a medium-sized manufacturing company based on an industrial estate which would be just within the proposed Congestion Charge Zone. The Congestion Charge would seriously affect your costs. You rely on road transport, because there is no rail freight depot nearby. Your delivery costs would increase considerably, as your lorries would be forced to pay the charge. Your suppliers' delivery costs would also rise, and they would pass on the costs to you. You and your sales team also have to use your cars every day for meetings with potential and existing customers, and with colleagues in other branches of the company. If the charge is introduced, you are sure the company will decide to close your branch. As your company is a major employer in the city, this is likely to result in a significant loss of local jobs. You may even lose your own job. The factory might be saved if you could persuade the Council to change the proposed boundaries of the charge zone to exclude the industrial estate. You would then only have to pay the charge for journeys into the city centre. THINK OF OTHER POSITIVE SUGGESTIONS YOU CAN MAKE.

Local resident

You live in the city centre with your spouse and two young children. Traffic in the city has increased enormously in the last ten years and now seriously affects your quality of life. You believe pollution from car exhausts is affecting your family's health. Both your children suffer from asthma, and you all suffer from various allergies and general poor health. Road accidents involving pedestrians in the city centre are increasing every year, and it is unsafe for your children to walk to school by themselves. Traffic noise is constant, and is a particular problem for you as you work shifts and often have to sleep during the daytime. Travelling around the city is very slow and difficult. You have considered moving out of the city to the suburbs, but accommodation there is more expensive, and travelling into the city for work would be very difficult. You feel very strongly that something must be done to reduce the number of vehicles on the roads – particularly private cars and heavy lorries. ARE YOU IN FAVOUR OF THE CHARGE?

Shopkeeper

You own a small mini-market on one of the main routes into the town centre. Your business relies on passing trade: commuters and lorry drivers stopping to buy snacks, drinks, newspapers and so on. Although you are well aware of the problems caused by traffic congestion as you have to drive to work yourself, you are worried about the effect that fewer people driving into and out of the city will have on your business, and on other small traders. You will have to pay the congestion charge yourself, as you need to use your van for your daily trip to the market. Your suppliers will also have to pay it, if they can't deliver before 8 a.m., so it will increase their costs, which they will pass on to you. You need to keep your prices competitive, but if your profit margins are cut much further your business will cease to make money. WHAT DO YOU THINK SHOULD BE DONE ABOUT THE CONGESTION PROBLEM?

Transport consultant

You are a transport consultant who has been asked to advise the Council on solutions to the traffic problem. It is very clear that traffic in the city has reached unsustainable levels. Traffic is causing very serious environmental problems: there is evidence of rising levels of diseases linked to air pollution; exhaust fumes and vibrations are also damaging buildings, and there is particular concern about some old buildings in the historic centre. Road accidents are increasing year on year, with pedestrians particularly at risk of fatal injury, and journey times through the city are getting slower. Considerable investment would be needed to improve public transport, which is slow and unreliable. The bus service is inefficient because of the congestion on the roads, and the railway network serves only some parts of the city. You believe the best option is to introduce the Congestion Charge, which, according to your research, should reduce traffic to more sustainable levels by discouraging unnecessary road journeys. The revenue generated by this scheme could be used to improve public transport. You believe the priorities should be to extend the rail service and increase subsidies to both buses and trains, in order to bring fares down to levels which would encourage more people to leave their cars at home. Alternative proposals have been suggested. Some are: build a bypass around the city, to reduce through-traffic; widen roads in the city centre, to let traffic flow more freely; build an underground railway. You are not in favour of these proposals. THINK OF OBJECTIONS TO THESE SCHEMES.

Environmentalist

You are an ecologist, representing an environmental campaigning group. You favour the Congestion Charge, but think the Charge Zone should be increased to cover a wider area of the city. Emissions of vehicle exhaust gases are now exceeding the limits recognised as 'safe' by the government. These pose a threat to human health – respiratory diseases and allergies are on the increase in the local population; the incidence of certain cancers is also higher than the national average, and many people suspect a link with air pollution in the city. You believe that the Council should use the revenue generated by the charge to fund improved rail and bus services. However, you believe the Council should go further than this. THINK OF YOUR OWN SUGGESTIONS.

Doctor

You are a general practitioner in the city, and you have to deal with the health effects of the traffic problem on a daily basis: road accident victims, respiratory diseases such as asthma, and various allergies. You suspect that pollution from road vehicles may also be responsible for some cancers which are becoming more prevalent. You also believe that an increase in stress-related conditions is partly due to the frustrations of getting to work. Traffic congestion is also a serious obstacle to you in going about your own work: apart from the problems of travelling to work, it is very difficult to make house-calls on patients who cannot come to your clinic. You feel very strongly that the Council must take action to improve the situation, but you have misgivings about the Congestion Charge. Emergency vehicles will, of course, be exempt from the charge, but you want an assurance that doctors will also be exempt. You are also concerned that the Congestion Charge will only discourage the less well-off from using their cars, and lead to further social polarisation. WHAT RECOMMENDATIONS WILL YOU MAKE?

Additional discussion point: The individual and the environment

Instead of a single ready-made task, here we are presenting some material (Texts 1–5) which you can use as a basis for discussion. We offer five different suggestions for ways of exploiting the material in discussion tasks (Plans 1–5, below).

Texts 1–5 are from a UK government advice leaflet designed to encourage individuals to reduce the impact they make on the environment. This is a concern that is likely to affect the more developed parts of the world more than less developed regions. If (some of) your students are from regions where the lifestyles of most individuals are responsible for very little pollution and waste, the texts (or some of them) could be used for comparison with their local situation, as in Plan 1, below.

Plan 1

Students read Text 1 and perhaps another extract (for example, Text 2), and discuss to what extent such advice would be relevant to their own country. They could discuss the level of environmental awareness in the population of their country/countries, and what kind of education is, or could be, provided to encourage public participation in environmental protection.

Plan 2 (suitable for a relatively short discussion)

Students read Text 1 only, and discuss what kinds of advice they expect the leaflet to contain. Optionally, they then design a leaflet.

Plan 3

As for Plan 2, but allocate each group one of the topics of Texts 2–4 ('at home', 'when you travel', etc.). They agree on the advice that should be included, and report to the class. They could be given the relevant text (or all the texts) as follow-up reading.

Plan 4

Depending on their reading level and the time available, students read either all or some of the texts. Some suggestions for discussion questions are as follows.

- How effective do you think the leaflet would be in persuading people to adopt more environmentally-friendly habits?
- Would the approach work in your country?
- What, if any, measures are taken in your country to reduce the environmental damage done by individual citizens?
- Do you take the environment into account in the choices you make in your daily life?
- How successful do you think such campaigns can be in minimising pollution, waste, and the depletion of non-renewable resources?
- Is this kind of campaign worthwhile, or would the money be better invested in developing cleaner technologies?
- Is the high-consumption, high-waste lifestyle currently enjoyed by industrialised nations sustainable, or must we all return to simpler, less extravagant ways of living?
- Apart from leaflets such as this, what methods could be used in a campaign to increase people's awareness of their impact on the environment?

Plan 5 (Jigsaw reading – a longer task)

Arrange groups of four (or three).

Step 1 (preferably set as homework): set all students Text 1 to read, and allocate each student in the group a different, additional one from the other four texts.

Step 2 (optional): students from different groups who have read the same text get together to check that they have understood the main ideas, and ask for help if necessary.

Step 3: form original groups of four/three; each student summarises the content of the extract they have read, and the others listen, take notes, and ask for clarification.

Step 4: discussion, as for Plan 4.

TEXT 1

"Pollution, wasting energy, wasting water, recycling. Not my problem!"

That's what many people think, but as individuals, we can all do things to help protect and improve our environment.

"But what can I do?"

Take local air pollution. You and your children could be at risk. Local pollution, such as car fumes, can aggravate asthma and cause premature deaths in those seriously ill. But you can help by, where possible, not using your car for short journeys, sharing car journeys with friends and family and having your car serviced regularly.

Pollution is also affecting the whole world. The burning of fuel in power stations and oil refineries provides you with the energy you use in your home and car. This burning of fuel also pumps out 'greenhouse gases' which cause global warming. In the UK this could mean more floods and storms, drier summers and wetter winters. You can do your bit to help the environment, and save money at the same time, by saving energy and resources.

"My life is too busy, I want convenience. Doing my bit for the environment has to fit into my lifestyle and budget."

It can – and you could save money too. A little thought about your everyday actions and how they affect the environment would really make a difference. Many people want to 'do their bit' for the environment but need advice on how to do it. This leaflet will help by giving you tips and ideas.

"Can I really make a difference?"

Yes, making a few changes in what you do at home, at work, when shopping or getting about is all that you need to do.

TEXT 2

doing your bit at home

Action to help our environment really does begin at home.
Here are some top energy and money saving tips for the home:

- Central heating – just turning down your thermostat by 1°C could cut your heating bill by 10%, saving you £15–£30 a year.
- Lights – remember to turn off any lights you don't need.
- TVs, computers and hi-fis – don't forget to switch these off too, if you're not using them.
- Washing machines – save water and energy by using a lower temperature wash or the economy programme and by washing a full load rather than half a load.
- Fridges – let food cool down before you put it in the fridge or freezer and avoid leaving the fridge door open for longer than you need.
- Kettles – if you're making tea for one, use just enough water for your cup of tea.

Here are some top tips:
- Report any water leaks you see to your local water company. If you have a water leak on your property, ask your water company whether it offers a subsidised repair service.
- Check all taps for drips and replace worn-out washers. A dripping tap can waste enough water in a day to run a shower for five minutes.
- Hot water – if your water is too hot, turn the thermostat down to around 60°C/14°F. Running hot water down the drain costs you money.
- Take a shower – it will use 2–3 times less water than a bath.
- Toilet devices – consider using a water-saving device in your cistern. They're often free from your water company and easy to install.
- Toilet flush – if you are replacing your bathroom, buy a dual flush toilet and use the short flush when you can.
- Avoid using sprinklers – if you do use them, your water company may wish to install a water meter and charge you for the water you use.

Is your rubbish rubbish?

Not everything you throw out this week will be rubbish.

Consider these facts:
- Producing new aluminium cans from used cans saves up to 95% of the energy needed to produce cans from raw materials.
- Every tonne of glass recycled saves over one tonne of raw materials like sand and limestone. This means less quarrying, less damage to our countryside, less pollution, valuable energy savings and less global warming.

Here are some top tips:
- Use your council's recycling scheme, if they have one.
- When you are going to the supermarket, make use of the recycling banks provided.
- Why not compost your garden and appropriate food waste?

Reducing rubbish is not just about recycling. You can also:
- Buy products with less packaging.
- Re-use items such as bottles, carrier bags and refillable containers.

And, protect your local environment:
- Bin your litter.
- Dispose of chemicals or oil in local authority facilities.
- Don't dump waste in water or on the ground.
- Don't try to flush away items such as nappies, condoms, or cotton buds. Bag it and bin it.

Doing your bit is easy

TEXT 3

doing your bit **when you travel**

We all travel – to work, to the shops and on holiday. For many, the car is essential.
Individual choice in owning a car is one of our greatest freedoms.

But this freedom comes with a price.

Consider these facts about emissions from vehicles:

- They make air quality worse.
- They contribute to acid rain and smog.
- They contribute to global warming.
- Pollution from car emissions can aggravate health problems such as asthma, and sitting in a car can result in you receiving up to three times more pollution than pedestrians.

Top travel tips:

- Walk when you can – it's great for your health.
- Cycle and enjoy the exercise. Take advantage of any designated cycle routes in your area.
- Catch a train or bus – family fares, ticket offers and group discounts mean public transport could cost less than you think. Contact National Rail Enquiries or your local bus company for further details.
- Park and Ride – these schemes are linked to priority bus lanes for a speedier journey, and take the hassle out of parking in town.
- Share car journeys with friends or family – the school run, journeys to work and shopping trips. Think about a car pool scheme with friends in your area.

Doing your bit when driving

- Keeping in tune: try to have your car regularly serviced. It will burn less petrol and emit less pollution. Under-inflated tyres can increase fuel consumption by up to 8%.
- Switch off – and save your petrol and money. Turn off your engine if it is safe to do so, especially if you're stuck in traffic for more than two minutes.
- Fuel efficient cars – ask your dealer about fuel efficiency between cars of similar specifications. The Vehicle Certification Agency produces a booklet outlining fuel consumption on all new car models each year.

You benefit

If you follow these tips you will feel the benefit straight away. Traffic congestion will be cut and so will your fuel bill.

Doing your bit feels good

TEXT 4
doing your bit **while shopping**

As a consumer you have choice and power through your spending decisions. Why not use it?

All the products you are buying will have some effect on the environment.
Are you doing your bit when shopping?

Here are some simple tips:

- Re-use bags or buy 'bags for life' which are now offered by most supermarkets.
- Choose good quality water-based or low-solvent paints, glues, varnishes and preservatives. They are less harmful to your health than solvent-based materials.
- When buying electrical products, choose the most energy efficient ones and reduce your electricity bills.

Ask your retailer to:

- Point out products made from recycled material such as plastic bottles (e.g. shampoos and soft drinks), kitchen rolls, tissues, toilet paper, writing paper and envelopes.
- Explain the environmental claims on products. If you don't understand, just ask. They should know.

Doing your bit matters

TEXT 5
doing your bit **at work**

Business has a major impact on the environment. All businesses use resources. Heating, cooling and manufacturing all use energy and add to global warming. The average office worker generates over half a kilo (more than 1lb) of scrap paper every day.

Here are some top tips:

If your company has a staff suggestion box or, via your union, encourage your employer to:

- Set up a car sharing scheme.
- Offer interest free loans for public transport.
- Buy recycled products.
- Promote a green bin policy so that you can easily recycle cans, glass and paper.
- Ensure machines and lights are switched off.
- Install flow controls in toilets – this is a rapid money saver and is good for the environment.

Doing your bit works

(Abriged from) Department for the Environment, Transport and the Regions. "Every little bit helps". London: Department for the Environment, Transport and the Regions, 1999. http://www.airquality.co.uk/archive/yourbit.pdf (8 January 2004).

Unit 6 Education
Questioning

> TO BE READ IN ADVANCE
> The research report extract for Discussion point 2 should be read before the lesson.

Useful language

Another problem with students' questions is often <u>grammatical</u>: a failure to use interrogative forms. This can result in questions being misinterpreted as statements if rising intonation is not used, or noticed: 'This is wrong?', intended as a comprehension check, might be misconstrued as an assertion. Malformed 'wh' structures (*What means...? How you call...?*) are also common. If appropriate, review question forms at the start of the lesson, or note problems for highlighting in feedback.

Discussion point 1: Choosing a university/college

Where possible, students should talk about their most current experience, such as choosing the institution they are or will be attending. The premise of this discussion is that the students have some choice in the matter; if this is not the case, they could talk about a previous choice (such as their undergraduate university, if they are postgraduates).

Discussion point 2: Assessment

Preparation 1

The report extract should be set to be read as preparation. The topic is also related to the Unit 7 theme, *Culture*. The content of the report may be of special interest to students who are going to be studying abroad. If your students are preparing for study in an educational culture that may be alien to them, you could ask them how much they know about the assessment methods that will be used. If they are already studying abroad, ask them to comment on their own experience: have the assignment/assessment types matched their expectations?

Preparation 2

Depending on your students and their context, you may find that the discussion of experience and expectations of assessment raises important issues of real concern to students. You may then feel these issues merit more class time than the *Discussion* questions, and you should adjust the timings accordingly (or drop the *Discussion* stage altogether).

In English-speaking university settings, the term *examination* normally refers to a major formal assessment, usually at the end of a term, semester or year; *test* refers to a smaller-scale, less formal check on progress, set during the term or semester. Students from some countries associate 'tests' with objective multiple-choice or short-answer formats, and 'examinations' with extended written papers, but we don't think the distinction is understood in this way in English-medium contexts.

Students from some European countries are used to examinations in which they are given several hours to write a long, detailed paper of many thousands of words. The typical situation in the UK, where students often have less than an hour to produce a relatively short essay, comes as something of a shock. They would need to adopt a very different approach to these short exams, in which careful use of time and conciseness are the key skills.

Debate

You could adapt Discussion point 2 as a motion for a debate – for example, 'Written examinations are the best way to assess students' or 'Written examinations should be abolished'.

Additional discussion task

Read the text (overleaf) about the launch of the UK's E-University in 2001. Here are some suggestions for questions to discuss.

- Have you any experience of studying by distance learning (using the Internet or older technologies)? If so, tell the group about it.
- What would be the benefits of studying for a degree at an 'e-university'? What disadvantages would there be?
- Would you consider taking a course by e-learning? Explain your answer.
- What types of student would be most likely to benefit from the establishment of e-universities?
- What do you think would be the important features of a successful e-university? In your group, draw up a list of what you think the priorities of an e-university should be.
- Do you think e-universities will ever take the place of conventional universities?

E-University goes online for postgrads

Joe Plomin

The E-University went online today for the first time, but only with three postgraduate courses.

Since early last year, the government has been predicting the new internet-based institution will rival organisations in the US and combine the best courses from around the UK in a single virtual educator.

But today's reality is a little more humble. After two years' work, it will be offering a module in an economics course at Cambridge, an MSc in information technology through Sheffield Hallam and an MA in public policy at the University of York.

The three announced today are to be used to test the new technology.

The interim chief executive of the new institution, Nick Winton, emphasised by next autumn, E-U could be offering other courses.

Students studying for a masters at Cambridge will complete a module through web-based learning, receiving their course material and support entirely through the internet. The Open University is contributing its experience as the main UK provider of internet support and resource material.

Similarly, the new postgraduate courses at Sheffield Hallam and York involve the institutions teaming up with organisations more used to the electronic provision of education.

The reason E-U is initially aiming at the postgraduate market is because it wants to attract the lucrative corporate market.

Sir Brian Fender, chairman of the E-U holding committee, is confident that eventually most universities will get involved in the national programme.

"We were delighted by the response from the higher education sector to our first invitation to submit proposals for programmes – over 80 different proposals from some 60 universities," he said.

The plan, according to Mr Winton, is the institution will be self-funded, with support from private industry. However, questions have been raised today about whether it can make money, given its first strategic deal, with a technology provider, has not involved any cash changing hands, and investors are wary about internet companies.

Plomin, Joe. "E-University goes online for postgrads." *Guardian Unlimited*, October 19 2001.
http://education.guardian.co.uk/elearning/story/0,10577,577321,00.html
(8 January 2004).

There is further material on the topic of e-learning in *Study Listening* (new edition), Unit 3.

Unit 7 Culture
Reporting

TO BE READ IN ADVANCE
It may take longer than usual to deal with the Useful language and the Practice exercise in this Unit, so you may need to allocate the texts for both *Discussion points 1* and *2* (Texts 1A and B, 2A to D) to be read in advance.

Useful language
The language presented here is relatively informal. More formal verbs which would be appropriate in writing, such as *states*, *holds*, *asserts*, *contends* may seem stilted or pretentious in the type of discussion most students are likely to be involved in.

Discussion point 1
Preparation 2 (pairs)
If you have an odd number, have two As or Bs in one group. They can share the task of explaining the term.

Discussion point 2
If your class is not divisible into groups of four, or if you need to reduce the time this task will take, use one or more groups of three or two. With groups of three, we suggest omitting Text 2C, as we suspect the 'masculinity/femininity' dimension may be less easy to grasp from this summary. If you need to have a group of two, use Texts 2A and 2B.

Additional discussion point: 'Culture bumps'
<u>Note</u> This list comprises a mixture of potential 'culture bumps' which might occur to people from Western anglophone cultures when they meet members of various other cultures, and vice versa. The list should, if appropriate, be adapted to suit the specific cultural situation of the students in your class, or a situation they are likely to meet in future.

Would you experience a 'culture bump' (Archer 1986) in any of these situations? If so, explain how you would feel, and why, and what – if anything – you would do or say.
1   Your teacher/lecturer sits on the desk throughout the lesson/lecture.
2   Someone you are eating with picks up food with his/her left hand.

3 You are eating dinner with someone who has a slight cold. They sniff continually throughout the meal.
4 Someone touches you on the head.
5 A friend comes into your house/flat without removing their shoes.
6 A stranger you pass in the street stares at you as you go by.
7 Someone you have never met before asks you what your salary is.
8 The person you're talking to keeps his/her head lowered throughout the conversation and avoids looking you in the eye.
9 Someone you know smiles at you and raises their hand with their fingers clenched and their thumb pointing upwards.
10 You decide to visit a student doing the same course as yourself. They talk to you briefly at the door, and tell you they are busy working on an assignment. They don't invite you in.

Unit 8 Globalisation
Dealing with questions

> TO BE READ IN ADVANCE
> You will need to allocate the texts for Discussion point 2 (Preparation 1) in advance. It will also save class time if students read the rather long Useful language section before the lesson, and the short text for Discussion point 1 (Preparation 1).

Useful language
Dealing with awkward questions
Our answer:
A You don't know the answer
  2 I don't really have any experience of that, but X might like to comment?
  3 I don't think there's enough evidence to say for sure.
  4 I haven't had time to look into that, sorry.
  5 I really don't know.
10 I'm not (quite) sure.
11 I'm not absolutely sure, but I'd guess that…
12 I'd need to think about that.
13 I've really no idea.
14 That isn't really my field, but perhaps X could say something about…?
16 That's rather out of my field.

B The question implies some criticism of your argument/research/understanding etc.

   1 I take it you don't think/believe/accept…?

C The questioner has misunderstood the issue

  19 Well, I think you'd be wrong to assume that…

  20 You seem to be assuming that…

D The question cannot be answered simply or briefly

  15 That's an important question, but it's really too complex to deal with now.

  18 There isn't really time to go into that now/here.

E You don't think the question is relevant to the discussion

   6 I think we should stick to the main issue here.

   7 I think we're going off the point a little.

  17 That's really a whole different argument/discussion/topic.

F You want to finish talking about something else before you deal with the question.

   8 I was just coming to that…

   9 I'll come back to that in a minute, if that's all right. I just wanted to…

Reasons for not knowing the answer

Our answers:

a) You have not thought about the issue before

   2 I don't really have any experience of that, but X might like to comment?

   5 I really don't know.

  10 I'm not (quite) sure.

  12 I'd need to think about that.

b) You have not read or remembered the information

   4 I haven't had time to look into that, sorry.

   5 I really don't know.

  10 I'm not (quite) sure.

  11 I'm not absolutely sure, but I'd guess that…

  13 I've really no idea.

c) The question has not been researched, or the research is inconclusive

   3 I don't think there's enough evidence to say for sure.

d) The question is outside your specialism

  14 That isn't really my field, but perhaps X could say something about…?

  16 That's rather out of my field.

Definitions:

'*off the top of my head*'

From memory, without checking.

'*gut feeling*'

An instinctive feeling, not based on careful consideration or study.

Discussion point 1

You may need to keep Discussion point 1 fairly short to allow sufficient time for Discussion point 2. Try to ensure this discussion does not pre-empt Discussion point 2.

Discussion point 2

Preparation 1

If your class is not divisible into groups of four, or if you need to reduce the time this task will take, use one or more groups of three. Text 2 is perhaps the most difficult both linguistically and conceptually, so with weaker groups, that may be the best one to omit.

Discussion 1

If you think your students will have difficulty with the texts, then we suggest that *before* Discussion 1, you get the students who have read the *same* text to get into groups and discuss the content, asking for your help where necessary. They should agree on what the main ideas are.

Discussion 2

If there is sufficient time and your students are relatively confident in discussion, create larger groups for this stage. But bear in mind the timing implications: six students should generate twelve questions.

Here are some 'standby' questions, in case your students have difficulty coming up with their own:

Questions related to extracts

Text 1

- Do you agree that globalisation is 'not primarily economic'?
- What have been the most significant effects of 'instantaneous global communication' in your experience?
- Is trans-national communication (Internet, satellite broadcasting) largely beneficial or harmful for your society?
- How can the potential dangers be minimised?

Text 2

- Has globalisation 'invaded' local culture in your experience? In what ways?
- In what ways is the influence of tradition declining in your/our society?
- What do you think Giddens means when he says 'you face much more of an open future'? Do you agree with that assertion?
- Are women in your/our society having to make decisions about their lives that their mothers and grandmothers did not face?
- Do you agree that there will be radical changes in the role of men? If so, how will it change?

Text 3

- Have you seen any evidence of the erosion of national sovereignty? Has it affected your country?
- Do you think the nation state will disappear, or do you agree with Giddens?
- Do big companies have too much power? Can they influence national politics?
- Do you think corporations have indirect access to *military* power?

Text 4

- Does 'globalisation' really mean 'westernisation'?
- What does 'westernisation' mean? What forms does it take?
- Do you think poor countries benefit from globalisation as much as the West?
- Should developing countries protect themselves from the damaging effects of globalisation? If so, how?

General questions

- Is globalisation a new phenomenon?
- Is it an inevitable trend?
- Should globalisation be resisted or encouraged?
- What are the positive and negative effects of globalisation?
- What can be done to reduce the negative effects?

Debate

Globalisation is a very suitable topic for a debate. One suggestion for a motion for the debate is: 'Globalisation is a positive force in the world'.

Additional discussion point

Preparation (individual)

Read the following comments.

'We live in a world where we have torn down walls, collapsed distances and spread information. The terrorist attacks on September 11 were just as much a manifestation of this globalisation and interdependence as the explosion of economic growth.'

Bill Clinton, Former US President

Now the world faces a big question. Is the type of globalisation which links the power of science and technology to a free market ideology going to make the whole world more peaceful? Or, as the [anti-globalisation] protesters fear, will it bring riches mainly to the few, new clashes between the haves and have-nots, development that places an unsustainable strain on the environment, and rage at the aggressive promotion of Western values? If they are right, is reform or radical change necessary to harness science and technology to a kindlier form of globalisation?

"The Chips are Down." *New Scientist*. 27 April 2002: 30.

Discussion

Do you agree with Clinton? What are your answers to the questions posed in the *New Scientist* extract?

Presentation skills

BACKGROUND NOTES

Objectives

The aim of activities in the *Presentation skills* component of Part 2 is to build up students' competence and confidence by giving guided practice in different aspects of presentation skills. These skills are then integrated in the more 'real-life' seminar presentations that are the core of the work in Part 3.

Design

The sequence of the eight selected skill areas is shown in the *Course Map* at the beginning of the book. The first four units provide a general basis on structuring, signalling, style, delivery and visual aids, and in these units students practise very short presentations (maximum 3 minutes) before presenting them. Units 5–7 provide a more detailed examination of the different phases of a presentation and Unit 8 is an overview. In Units 4–8, students prepare and present longer presentations (5–10 minutes).

The basic pattern of work in each unit of the *Presentation skills* materials is:

Introduction — Analysis — Presentation practice.

Of these unit sections, the *Introduction* is the most flexible. Below, we suggest various different ways it can be used according to the time available and your preferred teaching–learning approach. The other two sections (*Analysis* and *Presentation practice*) have set procedures built into the materials. You will find these are more detailed than the student materials for *Scenarios* and *Discussion skills*. Our intention is to make the procedures for these tasks clear to students as well as to teachers.

Each unit has short *Teaching notes* (pages 186–197), including suggestions for *Supplementary activities*. These provide more practice in the skill area that forms the main focus of the unit. If you have time, you can use the supplementary activities as extra practice in the *Analysis* section, before going on to the *Presentation practice*. Or you can use the supplementary activities for further practice, if the students' performance in *Presentation practice* indicates that more work is needed.

Topics

The topics for the presentation tasks in each unit have been chosen to suit a class of students from different countries, though not necessarily from different academic fields, which reflects the classroom mix on many pre-sessional courses. However, we realise that you may be teaching a group who share the same language/culture. When the topic in the students' materials is not suitable for a group who share the same language/culture, we suggest an alternative topic in the *Teaching notes*.

Procedure

Introduction

We recommend that, before the students read the *Introduction*, you elicit from your students as much as possible of the content. How much that will be possible will depend to some extent on the time you have available, and on how much experience your students already have in making presentations.

Students could be divided into groups of about four, to discuss points you take from the introduction; then spokespersons could report, for plenary discussion. If the content has been well covered at this stage, you could proceed immediately to the *Analysis* section, with students encouraged to read the *Introduction* outside class.

If coverage of the content has not been sufficient, then the *Introduction* should be read in class before going on to the *Analysis* section.

An alternative would be to ask students to read the *Introduction* before class, and then elicit the content from them, for informal discussion as well as checking understanding.

Analysis

In all units except Unit 4, the *Analysis* section makes use of recorded presentations, or extracts from presentations. These are on the CD (or cassette side A), and transcripts are provided on pages 205–211. The transcripts are intended to be used as a Key, after the *Analysis* task. However, if your students have difficulties in listening, it may be necessary to work from the transcript from the start.

Presentation practice

Preparation

This allows time for individual thought and planning. You may be asked for help with vocabulary or grammar. On the whole, try to restrict your advice to <u>language</u> points, leaving it to the listeners (at the *Practice* and *Presentation* stages) to react to and comment on the content and structure of their talk. This gives more meaning and purpose to the *Practice*, *Presentation* and *Evaluation* stages. Obviously, though, this is a matter of teacher judgement, and you may sometimes have to help or advise on content.

Practice (in Units 1–4)

For this stage, the students work simultaneously in parallel pairs. Move around the class, noting points for later comment. Encourage the students to take the initiative in requesting assistance. If it is possible for you to spread the students out into additional rooms or spaces, that reduces problems of noise interference between neighbouring pairs.

Presentation

For this stage, the students should form new groups (trios), since it is essential that each speaker presents their talk to a new audience. As before, the groups work in parallel.

Evaluation/Feedback

Most units contain *Evaluation* questions specific to the skill being practised. Give students plenty of time to think about their responses before you ask them to compare answers. After group discussion, ask for comments from the class as a whole. Finally, provide feedback on points you have noted at the *Practice* and *Presentation* stages which you think are worth bringing to the class's attention – positive as well as negative. Give priority to points relevant to the specific ground covered in that unit.

Summary

Each unit concludes with a *Summary*, to remind students of the core of the work covered in the unit. It is especially useful to review if you have had to spread the work over two separate lessons. You can, of course, use the summary as the basis for a fuller round-up discussion with the students.

Timing

We have designed the *Presentation skills* activities to take up 90 minutes (or two 45-minute lessons), but you may need to adjust the timing to match your students and your timetable. Below we indicate how, ideally, the distribution of time might work out, assuming two separate lessons of 45 minutes each.

For Units 1–4 (that is, those *with* a Practice stage):

Lesson 1	Introduction	20–25 min
	Preparation	5–10 min
	Practice	10–15 min
Lesson 2	Presentation	25–30 min
	Evaluation	15–20 min

For Units 5–8 (that is, those *without* a Practice stage):

Lesson 1	Introduction	15–20 min
	Preparation	10–15 min
	Presentation 1	15 min
Lesson 2	Presentations 2 and 3	30 min
	Evaluation	15 min

If your course schedule allows less than 24 hours (for all four Parts), or if your lessons last, say, 60 minutes instead of 45 minutes, you could ask the students to work through the Introduction and Preparation sections at home. It is in any case an advantage for them to have had the chance to mull over the ideas in advance. Begin the lesson by dealing with their questions about what they have read; then get them to talk over any Discussion points. Using homework in this way may enable you to complete the *Presentation skills* material in one lesson rather than two.

If your students are already fairly proficient in presentation skills, you could shorten the time spent on Part 2 in order to move to Part 3, *Class seminars*, where the format changes to longer presentations to the whole class.

TEACHING NOTES
Unit 1 Structuring your presentation

See page 184 of the *Background notes* for our suggestions for handling the introductory sections.

Being clear about your objective

If appropriate, ask the students about the objectives of presentations they have recently made or are likely to make (even if not in English).

Organising the information

Ask the students if they can think of any other ways of structuring a presentation, such as geographically.

Language signals

If you have time, you can ask students if they can think of any other language signals, and then look at *Checklist 3* on page 122.

Analysis

The transcript is on pages 205–206, with the signposts and language signals highlighted. We suggest that if possible you refer the students to it only after they have completed the second listening task. But if necessary they can use the transcript from the start.

Presentation practice

For general guidance see the *Background notes*. Make clear to the students the value of doing the presentation twice – the first time being a practice run that should help them to do it better the second time.

Supplementary activities

If you have time, take longer on the Planning stage. Have students plan their talk individually, then show it to a partner and discuss. They can practise with a different partner, and then present to another pair.

You could also spend more time on planning talks. You could ask the students to suggest topics, which you compile on the board. Have them discuss in pairs how they would organise talks on these topics (introduction, three main points, and conclusion). Then collect ideas, or trouble-shoot, in plenary.

Unit 2 Speaking in an appropriate style

See the *Background notes* (page 184) for ways of handling the introductory sections. If you have time, you can do more on formal and informal language features such as those shown in the table below.

Formal	Informal
passive voice	abbreviated auxiliary verbs
complex sentences with subordinate clauses	simple sentences or coordinate clauses
abstract nouns and nominalisations	lexis with general meaning (e.g. *thing, nice, get*)
words of Latin origin (e.g. *sufficient*)	words of Anglo-Saxon origin (e.g. *enough*)

Analysis

1 a) is more informal than b). b) is used in the recording.
2 a) is more informal than b). a) is used in the recording.
3 a) is more formal than b).   a) is used in the recording.
4 a) is more informal than b). b) is used in the recording.

The transcript is on page 206. The speaker's style is quite formal.

Again, if necessary, the students can work with the transcript while they listen. The important point to make here is that they need to be aware of formality and informality, and to achieve a balance that is appropriate for the context.

Presentation practice

See the Background notes.

This topic can be used even if your students come from the same country. They should listen for the ways in which similar content can be presented. They can imagine they are preparing the talk to present to other listeners.

A possible alternative topic: *Healthy Eating*.

Again, make sure the students recognise the value of doing the presentation twice, the first time being a practice run that should help them to do it better the second time.

Supplementary activities

If you have time, you could ask students to convert a short text in the active voice to the passive voice. For example:

We boiled the liquid for ten minutes and then we filtered it. We then froze the solids at -5 degrees Centigrade.

They could then compare the two versions for style, and discuss which would be more appropriate for each of the following:
a) a lab report
b) a conversation with a colleague in the lab
c) an academic presentation.

Opinions may vary! But it makes a useful talking point.

Unit 3 Delivery: Emphasis and phrasing

See the *Background notes* (page 184) for suggestions on handling the introductory section.

Ask the students to think about <u>listening</u> to presentations. Ask them about the difference between reading and listening. When reading, they can look back and re-read if they did not understand. When listening to an informal seminar presentation, it may be possible to ask for clarification; but if the presentation is formal, it is not possible to interrupt.

Explain the origin of *listener-friendly* (by analogy with *user-friendly*).

Phrasing

Read Text A <u>monotonously</u>, with as little phrasing and emphasis as you can. Do not vary your speed and intonation. It should sound very flat and unnatural.

Analysis

You could ask the students to rewrite the text in the same format as Text B above. Alternatively, they can divide the text in their books into phrases using slash marks (/) and underlining those words with the most stress.

There is no single correct version. The text can be interpreted in slightly different ways, which should become evident as soon as the students start discussing which words they want to emphasise. This is in fact one of the main points to make about phrasing and emphasis. Because it helps to communicate meaning, you have to know what meaning you want to communicate, and individuals may make different choices with this text. On the whole, they will work with 'idea units'.

As an example, you could write on the board: '*you have to know what meaning you want to communicate*' and then invite the students to divide it into phrases.

Accept or elicit the various possibilities.

you have to know / what meaning you want to communicate
you have to know / what meaning / you want to communicate
you have to know / what meaning / you want / to communicate

But point out that the following, for example, is unacceptable.

you have to / know what / meaning you want to communicate

If you like, have students start the Analysis task in pairs, rather than individually.

FIRST LISTENING

On the next page is a suggested answer. Accept slight differences of opinion, pointing out that some will hear very small changes of pitch as worth marking as stress while others may not consider it important enough. However, everyone should agree on the clearly marked phrases and stresses.

> **OK** / well what I'm going to do is **briefly** / describe the main **differences** between English and **Outlandic** / you should have in **front** of you two sets of **sentences** / with the English on **top** / and the Outlandic **underneath** / and what I'm going to do is to explain which **bit** goes with which **bit** / in each **language** / and to try to make clear the main **DIFFERENCES** between the **two languages**

Afterwards, point out to the students that the main message is not that there is a single right way to do it, but that it must be done, and meaningfully. The most common weakness among those presenting in English as a foreign language is a monotonous unmarked delivery, with almost equal emphasis on each word. This is boring to listen to, and more difficult to understand.

SECOND LISTENING
Rewind the cassette/CD to the beginning of the presentation.

The talk is based on a comparison of two sentences in English and Outlandic (a fictitious language). Write up the two sentences (shown below) – in both languages – <u>before playing the recording</u>. The students should write them down with plenty of space between Sentences 1 and 2 for their notes.

Sentence 1

| English: | *I have never eaten such a bitter orange.* |
| Outlandic: | *Commay aldri ooma laranja tow azeyda egu.* |

Sentence 2

| English: | *She is going there tomorrow evening.* |
| Outlandic: | *Vai imoron di noyt lah zee.* |

As they hear the talk, the students take notes on the main differences between the two languages. These are indicated on the transcript on page 207.

Draw attention to the structure of 'explaining' in the presentation. Each difference is first demonstrated and then summarised.

Presentation practice
Alternative topic: two different approaches to an issue, or two possible solutions to a problem, in the students' specialist area.

Supplementary activities

You could do more listening and analysis of Emphasis and Phrasing, using short extracts from any of the other recorded talks. (See the *Transcripts* for phrasing.) The talk from Unit 2 would be a good choice, especially if the students have heard it recently. The speaker uses very marked phrase groups, so it is quite easy to analyse. His phrase groups are also quite short on the whole.

You might like to discuss with the students how this is a contributory factor to his relatively formal style of speaking. Longer phrase groups are more typical of fast informal conversation. This is not a rule, but a tendency: the larger the audience, the more formal the context, with slower speed of speaking and shorter phrase groups – but still groups, not word-by-word delivery.

Unit 4 Using visual aids

Even if the students have no experience of giving presentations themselves, it should be possible to elicit responses on the basis of their experience as the audience. If the students have given presentations, they may have quite a lot to say on their experiences, preferences and problems. Note: There is more information in *Checklist 2* on page 120.

Analysis

Note: there is no listening activity in this unit.

See the suggestion in *Supplementary activities*, below, if you would like to do more than just follow the text in the students' materials. However, keep in mind that, compared with other units, you may need to allow more time for the preparation stage in the *Presentation practice* section, as the students have to make visual aids as well as plan what to say.

What kind of visual aid would you use?

a) a diagram
b) a bar chart or a table
c) text – well laid-out, for example with terms emphasised on the left and definitions either on the right or below
d) bar chart
e) line graph
f) pie chart
g) diagram
h) simple table
i) bar chart

Presentation practice

Note that the procedure here is slightly different from the procedure in other units. Students work in pairs initially, then work separately to make their jointly planned visual aid, and to plan what to say about it. Then their first practice is in the same pairs. Then, as in other units, they present to two different students.

It does not matter if the content of all the students' talks is very similar. It is unlikely to be identical, and students usually enjoy listening for similarities and differences. The fact that the content is similar also encourages more attention to language signals and mode of presentation.

Supplementary activities

The Analysis section could be supplemented by further vocabulary work: *x-axis, y-axis, line, curve, graph, bar, column, vertical, horizontal, shaded, hatched, open triangles and closed circles, rises, increases, peaks, falls, drops,* and so on.

You could get the students to convert a paragraph or two of text into a text slide.

If you feel your students are ready to try a longer presentation than in previous units, the activity in this unit could easily be extended, as follows.

PREPARATION The pairs of students could be asked to plan a complete talk of, say, 6 minutes, in which they will speak for 3 minutes each. They should plan an introduction, two or three main points, and a conclusion, as well as making up their two visual aids. They can practise with each other, with attention to appropriate style, phrasing and emphasis, and language signals.

PRESENTATION This could be done to the whole class. It may sound strange to do so when the topic is the same, but in our experience it works well as a training exercise, if done just once.

Unit 5 Introducing your presentation

(See the *Background notes* page 184 for ways of handling the introductory section.) If your students have not had much experience of presenting or of attending conferences, it might be best to deal with this in plenary, with a mixture of eliciting experience, telling them normal procedures, and inviting their opinions on what it is appropriate to include in an introduction.

Analysis

FIRST LISTENING

The last section of the recording is not the introduction but development of the first main point. You may prefer to stop the recording after the fourth point on the first listening, and then later play the rest just to show how the introduction merges smoothly with the body of the presentation.

1 and 2 The topic and four following main points are highlighted (italicised and underlined) in the transcript on page 208.
3 Other features typical of introductions are:
  - the greeting at the start
  - the indication that questions can be taken at the end of the presentation in the outline.

SECOND LISTENING

Collect the phrases on the board, and then make up a list of verbs: *present, give an overview, look at, continue by considering, you will see.*

You might like to draw their attention to this speaker's use of *I* and *we* and *you* in these phrases. These are stylistic choices that influence the relation of presenter and audience. The use of the first person singular pronoun is controlling and didactic; the first person plural pronoun is more friendly (colleague-to-colleague) and sharing. Using *you* involves the audience directly. This speaker uses a well-balanced mix, with more statement of authority at the start.

Presentation practice

Note that the presentation is longer than in previous units, and that there is no Practice stage. On the other hand, the Preparation stage is more complex, with a first phase of planning an outline for the whole talk, and a second phase of more detailed preparation of the introduction. You will need to circulate, give support and check on progress.

Make sure that the students understand clearly the procedure for the presentations, before they start. They have to use questions 1–4 as an evaluation checklist while listening to the introduction. You might like to put the questions on the board. Then, during the main part of the presentation, they must try to interrupt politely with a factual question.

Supplementary activities

After the second listening, you could ask the students to suggest more verbs useful for signposting in the introduction, such as: *describe, tell you about, speak about, argue, explain, discuss, summarise*. If you have time, this would be an opportunity to review the different grammatical constructions that follow these verbs.

The speaker uses clear phrasing and emphasis. You could give the students a short section to analyse, as in Unit 3. The transcript on page 208 provides a key for the phrasing.

Unit 6 Referring to visual aids

One possibility for introducing this Unit would be to show the visual aid on *Text as a visual aid*. Write it up on the board and simply read it aloud. Ask the students whether they thought it was a good presentation. Then present it again, expanding from the headings along similar lines to the expanded version shown in italics. Ask the students to evaluate that as well, and then move into discussion of the remaining points in the introduction.

Analysis

You will have to judge whether or not it is better for your students to have time to work with the Figure 2 flow chart before listening.

FIRST LISTENING

See the transcript on pages 208–209.

After the students have discussed their answers, you might like to tell them that the speaker who recorded the presentation felt uncomfortable with Figure 2, because she did not have enough time to deal with it. Normally she would have spent twice as much time on this visual aid, which has a lot of text on it.

SECOND LISTENING

The signals for focusing attention on the visual aids are indicated in the transcript.

Presentation practice

The procedure is much the same as in Unit 5. You may want to set a specific length of time for the questions after the presentations. If the class is large, allocate responsibility to one student in each group for controlling the question time.

Supplementary activities

- The recorded talk could be analysed further to see how the spoken presentation is linked to the visual aids. Students could identify the occurrences of words and phrases used in the visual aids and in the expansion.
- A section of the recorded talk could be analysed for phrasing and emphasis.

- The recorded talk could be appraised for level of formality. The style used for this presentation is standard acceptable academic speaking style, which is more informal than the style used in Unit 2.
- The flow chart could be used for another 'expanding from a slide' speaking activity. It could be divided so that some students work on one level of the chart, while others work on another level. Then they could present to each other.

Unit 7 Concluding your presentation

See our earlier suggestions (page 184) for ways of handling the introductory section. Emphasise the point (page 101) that they should not finish by simply saying 'That's all'.

Analysis

The recorded talk in this unit might be difficult for your students to follow. You should explain before they listen that it is the conclusion of a research seminar presentation, and therefore summarises what has been said earlier, which is not in the recording. Also, it has the most specialised content of all the recordings. The transcript is on page 210.

FIRST LISTENING

The students' materials state that the teacher will play the recording section by section, so that they can answer the questions one by one. This should give them support, and make the listening comprehension task easier. They are to take notes, check with a partner, and then check with you in plenary. Obviously, you can change this procedure to a straight-through listening if you think your students can manage it. Or you can give more support by playing each section a few times. If you think it is really too difficult as a listening exercise, have the students work with the transcript. The main purpose of the recording is not to develop listening skills but to provide a model for students to analyse.

SECOND LISTENING

Answers to task (b) are shown in the transcript on page 210.

Presentation practice

The students are all speaking on the same topic, though they are likely to say different things. We suggest therefore that questions are kept to the end of Stage 2, after all three presentations have been made. This gives the students the opportunity to take account of each other's points and arguments in their questions and discussion.

Summary

Use the summary for review and discussion.

Supplementary activities

- Listen again to the recorded talks in Units 2, 3 and 6, with special attention to the conclusions. (Note that the conclusions in these talks are much briefer because they are part of talks lasting 3 to 4 minutes.) Alternatively, this activity could be done using the transcripts.
- Have students, in pairs, draw up talk outlines, on any aspect of culture. Next, ask them to give their outlines to another pair, who then together write and present a conclusion.
- If your students have been having difficulty in keeping to time on their talks, this would be a good opportunity to discuss the problem. (See *Checklist 1* on page 119) They could then be asked to give short talks of specified lengths, concentrating on timing. They could speak in groups of four, taking turns for one person to monitor the timing. The time monitor should give a warning when there is only one minute left, and stop the talk when the time is up, finished or not.

Unit 8 Making it interesting

Analysis

This is the longest of the recorded talks, but it is clearly delivered. We think it's interesting! The transcript is on pages 210–211.

SECOND LISTENING
See the transcript for:

surprising statistics	the thousand dollar bills (paragraph 2 in the transcript)
personal anecdote	in Papua New Guinea (paragraph 4 in the transcript)
vivid examples	Coca-Cola, Benetton's etc. in the shopping mall (paragraph 3 in the transcript) and very many more
analogy	no example
quote	Castell at the end

Presentation practice

If possible, allow some time for the self-evaluation discussions at the end. This should help the students review everything they have learned, and realise their own strengths and weaknesses, so that they can focus in the future on what needs improvement.

You may need to circulate during these discussions, to encourage those who are overly self-critical to realise that at least some of their presenting skills are satisfactory.

Supplementary activities

The recorded talk in this Unit could be used to review all the work done in Units 1–8. This would best be done at the end of the *Analysis* activities. Students could make up an outline and annotate with the language signals used in each section. They could analyse it for phrasing and emphasis. You could get them to evaluate the speaking style, and level of formality.

If time presses, the self-evaluation task at the end could be done in just a few minutes. However, it could be usefully extended to a more substantial activity. Each student could give a 'plus' or 'minus' rating for each aspect, for themselves and for the others in the group. They could then circulate the ratings amongst themselves and discuss. This could lead to a profitable review and discussion, whole-class, about the acquisition of presentation skills – and the need for practice.

Class seminars

TEACHING NOTES

Part 3 provides the basis for as many cycles of seminars as you have time for in your course. You can adjust the length of the individual seminars to suit your timetable. In the students' Overview (page 118) we have assumed a 30-minute seminar (10 minutes each for presentation, discussion and feedback). That would allow two students' seminars in an hour's lesson, or three in a 90-minute lesson. If your lessons are only 40–45 minutes, then you might extend the timing so that each lesson is devoted to a single seminar (15–20 minutes for presentation, 15 minutes for discussion and 10 minutes for feedback).

The **Rehearsal** stage is particularly important. Time management is often a problem for less experienced presenters, who tend to prepare too much material. So rehearsing will give them a realistic idea of how long their material will actually take to deliver. They can then cut it down before the seminar to what can be covered in the time available.

Feedback

During the seminar, make notes on the points (positive as well as negative) that you want to mention to the presenter at the end. Do the same for the questions and discussion that follow the presentation. You may want to use the *Seminar evaluation form* (pages 200–201) as a note-frame for your comments. You will need to have a stock of copies ready for each session.

At the end of the discussion, give out the copies of the form to the class. While the other students are completing it and writing their comments, take the presenter aside to give feedback based on the notes you have taken. We usually talk to the presenter in the corridor outside the classroom, or in an adjoining room. This is for two reasons: firstly, giving feedback one-to-one is less threatening than it would be in front of the class; secondly, it means that your opinions will not directly influence the evaluation comments from the rest of the class.

We have found that a good opening gambit for the feedback is to ask the presenter whether they would do anything differently if they were going to give the presentation again. Invariably, the presenter is already aware of things about their talk that went less well than they had expected. Then select points that you want to mention; there will probably not be time to cover all of them.

When you have talked to the presenter, go back to the class and spend a couple of minutes comparing their responses to the final set of *Questions and Discussion* items on the form (items 15–20). This helps remind them that both presenter and questioners contribute to the success of a seminar. At the end of the seminar slot, we collect in the completed forms, skim-read them to get an overall impression of how well they think the presenter and questioners did, and then pass them on to the presenter at the end of the lesson. If you give them back during the lesson, the presenter will probably read the forms and not pay full attention to the next student's presentation.

Recordings

If you can video- or audio-record the seminars, you may want to use short excerpts from the tapes for more detailed feedback, either in class (for example, *Proof-listening* on pages 143–144) or as an independent study activity (for example, the *Speaking Log* on page 155).

Seminar evaluation form

For each item, circle the comment that expresses your opinion or write in your answer.

THE PRESENTATION

1 What was the **best aspect** of the presentation?

2 Were you able to follow the presenter's **main points**?   YES   WITH DIFFICULTY   NO

3 Was the presentation **well-organised**?   YES   GENERALLY   NO

4 Did the presenter show when s/he was **starting a new point**?   YES   GENERALLY   NO

5 What about the presenter's **visual aids**?
   Were they clear?   YES   GENERALLY   NO
   Did you have enough time to read the information?   YES   NO
   Was the print large enough?   YES   NO

6 Comment on the **speed** of speaking: TOO FAST   TOO SLOW   JUST RIGHT

7 Was the presenter's **voice** loud enough?   YES   GENERALLY   NO

8 Were there any **technical terms** in the presentation that you didn't know?   YES   NO

9 Did the speaker **explain** the meaning of those terms?   YES   SOME OF THEM   NO

10 What about the **quantity** of information?   TOO MUCH   TOO LITTLE   JUST RIGHT

11 Did the presenter make enough **eye contact** with you?   NO   YES

12 Have you any comments on the presenter's **positioning** or **body language**?

13   Did the presenter give a clear **conclusion**?   YES   NO

14   What advice would you give the presenter for her/his next seminar?

THE QUESTIONS and DISCUSSION

15   Did you **understand** all the questions from listeners?   YES   NO

16   If not, **whose question(s)** were hard to understand – and why?

17   How well did the presenter **handle the questions**?   VERY WELL   OK   NOT VERY WELL

18   Did the speaker **avoid** answering any questions?   YES   NO

19   Did anyone **disagree** with the presenter?   YES   NO

20   Did you understand the **reason for their objection**?   YES   NO

Strategies for success

Improving your speaking outside class

TEACHING NOTES

The aim of this end-of-course session is to stimulate students' thinking about 'life after the course' and ways of making further progress in their spoken English without access to the usual support system that the language classroom provides. In a broader sense it should help develop autonomous language learning. There are two sorts of task. The three Discussion Tasks encourage the students to express their attitudes and beliefs about learning English, and the four Practice Tasks give them the opportunity to try out the strategies suggested.

We have adapted some of the material from *PROFILE – Principles, Resources and Options for the Independent Learner of English* (Anderson and Lynch 1996). The session is intended to be <u>exploratory</u>, providing the opportunity for individuals in a class to compare their experiences as language learners and to gain from those of other international students. It should not be seen simply as a checklist of 'tips' presented by *us* (teachers) to *them* (students). We prefer to think of what we aim to do in this session as 'learner education' rather than 'learner training' in a narrow sense. If you would like to know more about the background to the *PROFILE* project and its rationale, see Lynch (2001b).

The main point we want to get across to our students is that no single technique for learning a language *guarantees* faster progress. A secondary but important point is that language teachers are not the only source of guidance and expertise; their fellow language learners are perhaps better placed than anyone else to pass on their insights into useful strategies for independent learning.

Discussion and comparison of learning experiences gives us a wider range of options which we might adopt or adapt for our own purposes. In this spirit, we hope you and your students will find the *Strategies for Success* materials a useful springboard to discussion. Feel free to adapt them to suit the English learning context in which you are working. The notes below represent our responses to the issues raised in the various Tasks, and should not be taken as the only solutions.

Discussion task 1

	Problem	Reason
First student	*little chance to speak; self-expression*	*Italian/English differences; tends to think in Italian*
Second student	*pronunciation (vocabulary)*	*unfamiliarity of phonetic system*
Third student	*speaking and listening; loss of confidence*	*different accents*
Fourth student	*self-expression*	*lack of vocabulary*

Practice task 1

The idea of this task is firstly to put the students into a situation in which problems of expression should arise, leading in a natural way to the need to adopt communication strategies. Secondly, it should highlight the fact that collaboration between listener and speaker is the key to sorting out the problems.

Practice task 2

This task is intended to encourage students to focus on the role of syllable stress as part of a word's identity. There are interesting discussions of the role played by stress in comprehensibility in the books by Dalton and Seidlhofer (1994) and Jenkins (2000). Jenkins argues that the role of stress in international communication is a grey area, and that correct stress placement probably matters more when talking to native listeners than to fellow international students. We think it is important to point this out to the students if you are teaching in an ESL setting.

Discussion task 2

Our answer is given in the paragraph following this task.

Practice task 3

This task is more involved than the others, but can be done individually and could be set as a homework task. It will probably take about 30 minutes to complete. If you find that, having tried out the 4-3-2 technique, your students say it isn't helpful, it may be worth exploring their reasons for saying so. We have heard students (and teachers) comment that the task is unnatural. That itself can lead on to useful discussion: can a language learner benefit from a task that isn't natural?

Practice task 4

For this task to work really well, make sure the students keep to the 'only once' rule. Don't allow any speakers to repeat or clarify, and don't allow the listeners to compare what they are writing as they are writing it!

We think it's also important to put yourself in the same position as the listeners. Write down what *you* understand of each speaker's statement. We usually find that, although the teacher is able to decipher every student's sentence, the students have difficulties with each other's. Ask them what conclusion they draw from that.

Some students may realise that if they say their sentence V–E–R–Y S–L–O–W–L–Y, they stand a better chance of being understood. If this happens in your class, you can then discuss with the students what the penalties of speaking like that in real life would be!

Discussion task 3

This is obviously an open question. We hope your students will suggest ideas you find interesting and useful.

Transcripts: Presentation skills *extracts*

1 WORK AND FAMILY LIFE

signposts are italicised and underlined
signals of examples are italicised

<u>*today / I'm going to focus on a particular aspect*</u> of work / often called the work-family balance debate / by this term work-family / we mean the way in which people combine or juggle their paid employment and the rest of their lives / *which might include* the care of children or of elderly parents /

in the literature you often see other similar terms used / *such as* the work-family interface / or / perhaps the reconciliation of work and family / and the discussion of things called family-friendly policies / and *these might include* maternity and paternity leave / flexi-time / perhaps compassionate leave / for the care of dependants /

the term the reconciliation of family and work / actually comes from the European Union / and the EU's interest in and concern about this issue / has been responsible of course for generating a lot of funding / and more research and more policy in this area / you'll notice when you're reading some of the key texts in this area / that much of the research compares work-family balance in / say one Western European country / with another Western European country / or perhaps with North America / *for example* frequently in the British literature / it's said that / in Britain there are the highest weekly working hours in Europe / with an average of 48 hours a week / of course that may be high compared to / *say* Norway / but it's not so high if you make global comparisons / and <u>*we'll be looking at this in more depth next week*</u> /

<u>*today though / I want to focus in on one neglected aspect*</u> of the Western European and North American literature on work-family balance / and that is children's perspectives and opinions / when the interest in work-family balance began / researchers tended to focus on the experiences and opinions of parents and of employers / and increasingly commentators are drawing attention to the missing voices of children in the work-family debate / *for example* there was an extensive review of the reconciliation of work and family life for men and for women / in 15 countries in Europe / which was carried out in the mid-1990s / by Deven and colleagues / and Deven and colleagues highlighted this absence of knowledge about what children thought and felt / and they emphasised the importance of gathering the views of everybody / including children and young people / about the world of work / and work-family relationships /

for two years at the end of the 1990s / I was part of a research team which did just that / we used the oil and gas industry as a case study / and interviewed a wide range of people about work-family balance / and that included employers / health professionals / teachers / parents / and children / so we discovered that / if appropriate research methods were used / children could certainly contribute to the work-family debate / they could communicate their experiences and opinions / *including* how their parents' work impacted on their lives / and what their own aspirations were for work and family life /

the research methods we used involved 8–12-year-old children mainly / and we carried out group interviews / with their peers in school / and then follow-up interviews / either individual interviews or with their family / we developed information and consent leaflets and a range of games and activities / and also used drawing and writing techniques /

now I'm going to explain these in more depth / and then outline our results / and then we'll conclude today's session with a group activity / and I'll get you to discuss whether these research methods and research questions are applicable in your own home countries / or whether they could be adapted or you would use just different methods altogether / *but before we go on to this though / we'll take a short break*

(3 min 47 sec)

2 GENETICALLY MODIFIED FOOD

phrases used or adapted for the Analysis task are italicised
signals and signposts are italicised and underlined

I'm going to talk to you today / about some of the concerns / over the effects of using genetically modified organisms / in the production of food / *now the problem with these new plants and their widespread use / is now only just being discovered / for example* in Mexico they recently discovered that pollen from herbicide-resistant corn / had spread hundreds of miles from the original site where it was first planted / and this discovery runs directly counter to the claims of the scientists / that cross-pollination would not take place / beyond a few hundred metres from one of these new crops /

why then are we taking risks / with these novel organisms in the environment / *well of course* the great claim that is made for these products / is that they represent the only way / in which we will be able to feed the hungry in years to come / *the growing human population is projected to peak at around 10 billion / sometime in the 21st century / this greatly enlarged population will require increased farm outputs* / and according to companies like Monsanto / genetic engineering / will enable farmers to triple crop yields / without requiring any additional farmland /

however if we *actually* look / at the causes of famine around the world / we know from studies in India and Ethiopia / from the Sahel and from Bangladesh / that famines / on the whole / are not caused by absolute shortages of food / *indeed* / at the very time that Ethiopians were themselves in the midst of a most horrendous famine / in the late 1980s / it turns out that their government was still exporting 50% / of the food produced / on the land there / so devoted are governments around the world / to the new global market in food / the real cause of famine / is that in the new global food market / it is those without cash / money / to buy food / who have the worst diets / and suffer in famines /

so then we find that it is the distribution of cash / in a global economy / rather than the quantity of food that is grown / that is the real cause of food poverty / and it is likely *of course* / that genetically engineered organisms / belonging as they do in terms of their patents to large corporations / will *actually* only enhance the problems of the 'cash-poor' / in gaining access to a decent diet

(2 min 55 sec)

3 COMPARISON OF ENGLISH AND OUTLANDIC

the four main differences are italicised and underlined

OK / well what I'm going to do is briefly / describe the main differences between English and Outlandic / you should have in front of you two sets of sentences / with the English on top and the Outlandic underneath / and what I'm going to do is explain which bit goes with which bit / in each language / and to try to make clear the main differences between the two languages /

OK so the first sentence 'I have never eaten such a bitter orange' / is in Outlandic 'commay aldri ooma laranja tow azeyda egu' / now to translate that word for word / 'commay' is 'ate' / A T E / 'aldri' is 'never' / 'ooma' is the indefinite article that would be 'a' or 'an' in English / and 'laranja' is 'orange' / 'tow azeyda' is 'so bitter' / and 'egu' is 'I' / so if we were to give a word-for-word translation / that would be / 'ate never an orange so bitter I' /

if you look at the second sentence / 'she is going there tomorrow evening' / that would be in Outlandic / 'vai imoron di noyt lah zee' / 'vai' for 'goes' / 'imoron' 'tomorrow' / 'di noyt' 'at night' / 'lah' is 'there' and 'zee' is 'she' / so the word-for-word translation would be / 'goes tomorrow at night there she' /

OK so those are the two example sentences / so / what are the main differences / well firstly you can see that in the sentences we have 'egu' at the end of the first one / and 'zee' at the end of the second one / *so the subject pronoun / normally comes / at the end of the sentence in Outlandic* / *whereas in English of course it's at the beginning* /

the second difference is that / if you look at the first sentence you have 'such a bitter orange' / in English / and 'ooma laranja tow azeyda' in Outlandic / so you see that *the adjective in English comes before the noun / whereas in Outlandic it comes after the noun* /

the third difference / if you look at the first sentence again / you'll notice in Outlandic there are three words which all have A / the letter A at the end / 'ooma' /'laranja' / 'azeyda' / and in fact the letter A at the end indicates a feminine noun / so 'laranja' is feminine / and that causes the article 'ooma' / and the adjective 'azeyda' / to agree with it / *so a third difference between English and Outlandic is that in Outlandic you have grammatical agreement between articles nouns and adjectives* /

right so the fourth difference / I want to look at / looking this time at the second sentence you can see that in English we have / 'there tomorrow evening' / but in Outlandic that becomes / 'imoron di noyt la' / 'tomorrow at night there' / *so in Outlandic adverbs of time / come before adverbs of place / but it's the other way round in English* /

so of course those are not the only differences / but they are four of the main differences / between the two languages

(3 min 43 sec)

5 ORGANIC FARMING AND THE ENVIRONMENT

topic and following main points are italicised and underlined

good morning / in today's seminar / I will be presenting *the effects of organic farming on the environment / and biodiversity within the United Kingdom's ecosystems* /

organic farming has long been held as friendly towards the environment / but only recently / has long-term research become available / before delving too deeply into the topic / I'll give a *brief overview of the principles which define organic farming in the UK* / this will include details / of not only practices on arable organic farms / but upland grazing areas as well /

we will then look at the data recently published concerning the environmental impacts of organic farming / the data consists of carbon dioxide and methane omissions / levels of nitrogen run-off in water / and erosion /

I will continue by considering biodiversity / measured by bird and insect populations / rare flora abundancy / and soil micro-organism numbers / on organic farms within the UK / much of the data is comparing population levels on organic farms / to population levels on conventional farms / farms within the research were chosen for having similar areas of farmed land / the same or comparable crops / and being within the same region of the UK /

finally while you will see most of the research supports organic farming as being beneficial / it is important to recognise / there may be some organic practices that could potentially be harmful / to both the environment and biodiversity / for example / the practice of using peat as a soil additive to build up organic matter /

afterwards / I will be more than happy to take / any questions you may have /

the principles of organic farming have been defined by the United Kingdom Register of Organic Food Standards / also known as UKROFS / as the following / to work with the natural systems rather than dominating them / to encourage biological cycles involving micro-organisms / soil flora and fauna / plants and animals / to maintain or develop valuable existing landscape features and habitats for wildlife / with particular regard for endangered species / to pay careful attention to animal welfare considerations / and finally / to consider the wider social and ecological impact of the farming system

(2 min 10 sec)

6 ASSESSMENT IN EDUCATION

signals to the visual aids are italicised and underlined

I'd like to focus on assessment / the process of assessment / at whatever level in a course / and whatever education system / whether universities / or primary school levels or / the full range /

and if we ask ourselves *the first question there / on my slides / question A / for what purposes* / why do we do this / why do we bother spending so much energy and resources assessing our students /

we can think of it in two different senses / firstly _if we look on the left / in the summative sense_ / we like to categorise our students / we like to put a grade on each of our students / we can think about / for example / separating stronger students from weaker students / if it's for example about pushing some of the stronger students along in the system / we're keeping the weaker students back / and if we then think about / another sense in which we can assess our students / _the formative way / on the right-hand side there_ / that would be more in the sense of providing a chance for feedback / not only for the student / because they would like to see how they're doing and they know where to spend their energy / doing more studying and so on / also from the tutors' or the teachers' point of view / they could then spend more time with certain weaker students and so on /

for whatever purposes / _if we move on down the slide_ / we have to be aware that the process of assessment changes the relationship between the student and the teacher / it establishes a hierarchy / now the teacher has a certain power over the student / and that happens whether the assessment takes place for formative / or summative purposes /

now / _leave that bottom bit on the slide_ / and think about / how we can address this power imbalance / and I think / _if we look at this flow chart here / we see_ that what the assessor gets involved with / the marking and commenting / _is away down the chart / it's a flow chart that shows you that_ / if an assessor is going to do his or her job well / then marking and commenting is _only number 3 there / which is away down the chart_ / and they have to do a good job well before it comes to marking and commenting / there's a lot of ground work to do / _there up number 1 for example / that left box there_ / they have to check / and see whether the student actually understands what the ground rules are / and the scheduling / when is this work to be handed in and so on / so that when it comes to marking / _way down the bottom_ / they actually know that it was 20 marks off for handing it in a week late and so on / not only requirements in ground rules / also we have to know / what the students' strategies will be / so that when they all go for books / or resources they need for sitting their test / they need to be able to have all these books available and so on at the right time / and that covers more or less the groundwork /

briefing and advising students needs to be done well / they need to / we need to be clear ourselves about / when we are going to advise them / how much up to what point before the assignment we are going to do this / how we're going to cover all the students equally / and so on

so a lot of work to be done / before the marking and commenting / _and if we go back to our first slide_ / that is really about / making the whole process of assessment a lot more transparent / and I would argue / if we want to minimise the chances for abusing our power over the student / and if we want to minimise / the kind of power relationship / and the negative effects of that / then there is a need for transparency in that full process

(3 min 22 sec)

7 MASS MEDIA AND THE SPREAD OF AMERICAN ENGLISH

verbs and verb phrases used to report the academic inquiry are in italics

so / in this paper / we've *evaluated* a number of arguments / both for and against the idea / that there's some kind of global cultural norm / or global linguistic norms / that are being spread by the mass media /

we've *looked at* evidence from lesser spoken varieties of English / like New Zealand English / and *evaluated* the evidence for transfer / of US English variants / into those varieties / we've also *considered* the possibility that there is an effect that the media is having / on people's attitudes towards / dialectal varieties of American English /

in general / though / the main point of the arg- of the paper has been to *propose* that we / need to have more rigorous triangulation of the issues involved here / and when we *are evaluating* the supposed effects of the media on / any regional varieties / we need to both *take into consideration* typological factors / that is we need to *be alert* to the actual linguistic structure of the varieties involved / we also need to *take into account* sociolinguistic research / such as factors to do with the distribution / of the variants that we're *looking at* / but perhaps most importantly / we also need to *pay attention to* the attitudes of the speakers within any local community /

the regional culture / or the very local culture / of a speech community / clearly interacts with / any supra-local issues that are going on / any supra-local movements that are going on / and we think that / in fact / what we're going to *find* / as we *look closer at* this phenomenon / is that we're going to *see* that the media may in fact be the vector for transmitting quite simple amounts of information / but that when we're *considering* the kind of really complex knowledge that's involved with *looking at* linguistic variation / we're going to *see* proof that what's required is very close face-to-face communication between individuals / and that that kind of cultural contact over-rides any of these other supra-local factors /

(1 min 55 sec)

8 GLOBALISATION

globalisation is a term that we hear more and more about these days / protestors at recent economic summits in Milan and Seattle / have condemned globalisation as something that affects all of us in a negative way / social commentators increasingly use the term to describe social economic and political change in the modern world / but what does globalisation actually mean / what do sociologists have to say about it /

I think we can reduce globalisation / to four or five main trends / the first / and probably the most well-known / with which people are familiar / is the exponential growth / of amounts traded on world stock and capital markets / and with that / the implication that economic change in different parts of the world / affects us all / a graphic example of this is given by Tony Giddens in a recent book / where he suggests that / were the amount of financial transactions conducted on a daily basis / to be totted up in terms of piles of thousand dollar bills / those piles would themselves be thousands upon thousands of miles high /

a related aspect of such economic globalisation / is the way in which / increasingly markets are dominated by global products and brands / no matter where we go in the world we can find Coca-Cola / Benetton / McDonald's / Sony / Ford / and so on / it's been suggested / that were we to be dropped into a shopping mall in Western Europe or North America / and not know which country we were in / it would be very difficult to tell from the shops round about us / where in fact on the planet we were /

a third important aspect / is the growth of information technology / and the prospect that holds out / of instant global communications / the Internet / phones / broadcasting / cinema / this means that news / travels around the globe at the speed of light / the twin towers disaster / was knowledge / around the world within a matter of minutes / or hours / Hollywood / leads to global culture / films made in America receive a widespread audience across the globe / in almost no time / I have personal experience of this / about ten years ago I visited a very remote village in Papua New Guinea / it could only be accessed by plane and by travelling along a dirt track / the village had no running water, and no electricity / all the village was gathered round a generator / watching Rocky IV / on a television monitor /

alongside this of course / we have the growth of a world language / English / the language of business and the most powerful state in the world / the United States of America /

a fourth dimension of globalisation / is the recognition of environmental risk / the ecological impact of industrialisation / no longer respects national frontiers / the Chernobyl disaster / when a nuclear reactor in Russia exploded / might have been a problem for the Russians / but it was also a problem for the whole of the rest of the world / which suffered the impact / of radiation contamination / our access to cheap power in the West / may also mean / the expansion of the Sahara desert in North Africa / or increasing floods in China / or Latin America / or Central Europe / global environmental and climate change / reminds us / that we have to find a way to take responsibility / for our local actions / which often have global implications /

this brings me to the last aspect of globalisation / the rise of identity / reflexivity / disenchantment / and radical doubt / what do sociologists mean by those rather obscure terms / they simply mean that / in the modern world tradition / religious belief / and established authority / no longer exert the control over people's lives / that they once did / our greater personal freedom however / also means / a rise in a bewildering number of choices / about how we ought to live / as Manuel Castells / the well-known Spanish sociologist / has argued / our societies are no longer like orderly prisons / they are more like disorderly jungles

(4 min 27 sec)

Transcripts: *Sample* scenario *performances*

Scenario 4 Deadline for an essay
Sample 1: **Native speakers**
T = Tutor   (female, English)
S = Student   (male, Scottish)

T oh hello Pasquale / did you want to speak to me about something?

S good morning yes I'm sorry I won't take up...much of your time / I was just wanting...

T I've only got about ten minutes actually

S oh right so

T I've got a meeting

S I'll I'll be quick / yeah it was just about the essay that um is supposed to be handed in tomorrow

T hmhm

S at five o'clock

T that's right

S um...I've had some problems with um one specific book

T oh dear

S um that I've had to use in the essay it's one of the main sources for the book

T hmhm

S and um the only copy there was one copy at the university library / typical / and it had been borrowed by another student and uh / I asked for it to be recalled about a good two weeks ago / and um it only came back to the library yesterday and usually these...when it's recalled they have to bring it back within a week but

T hm

S obviously this student hasn't heeded this and uh has kept it for...uh for an extra week

T uhuh I see

S uh I'd really need to sort of...take time to read and you know analyse all the information

T but um Pasquale...your first essay was late as well wasn't it? / I mean

S yes that's right

T this is your second essay

S yeah yeah

T of the whole course

S yeah that wasn't…

T your first one was late I gave you an extension that time

S uhuh

T because you were ill

S yeah yeah

T and you bought me a…you brought me a medical certificate

S I did yeah

T and that was fine

S that's quite right

T but I mean this is your second essay and you're asking for another extension I don't think…

S hmhm

T I don't really think I can do that

S yeah in fact I feel quite bad you know…asking asking for it because you know I do appreciate that I have already asked for an extension / I mean two extensions you know for…yeah for one person

T uh for two

S exactly but I mean I reckon I should be able to finish the…the essay by Sunday I know perhaps it's not um that good but um I should be…

T well

S able to hand it in by Monday / would uh I know there's a…there's a…

T well I have a rule that if you hand it in after the deadline if there isn't…um you know if it isn't a special case

S right yeah

T exceptional circumstances then um then I have to take ten per cent off the mark that I give you

S hm

T so you really have to um you really have to weigh up um whether you think you're going to gain more than ten per cent

S hmhm

T in marks by having this extra time really don't you?

S yeah yeah I mean that's right but I mean this / I don't mean to…keep talking about it but this particular source was…hm perhaps the most important with…there was another book as well which I have…but this particular book was one of the most important sources / I mean I know we shouldn't rely on just one one source

T no no

S but um this was particularly important it's one of the key books on the subject you know

T hmhm / you say you recalled it two weeks ago?
S recalled it two weeks ago and it's supposed to be back you know
T yes yes
S within a week but it wasn't and they kept it for another week
T but um but Pasquale this is February
S hmhm
T yeah? / you've had those essay titles
S hmhm
T uh we gave you all the um assignment titles at the beginning of the course
S hmhm
T so / I mean / don't you think it was a bit late to recall a book
S hmhm
T two weeks before the deadline?
S in fact it was…it it's partly my fault because I did…get hold of the book as soon as the essay titles came out / I wasn't sure what title to to do
T hmhm
S and I…I got this particular book out and I made some photocopies from it
T hmhm
S but uh I didn't get the the articles that I actually need for this particular essay / 'cause I was working on a…initially I was working on another question
T I see
S and I switched questions
T yes yes um well I mean if you…you can have until Monday as long as you accept the ten per cent losing the ten per cent
S hmhm
T but it seems to me a great pity
S hmhm
T um because I I you know I think if you if you really worked very hard between now and five o'clock tomorrow…I mean I presume you've done most of the work already?
S oh yes the the bulk of the work I have done definitely
T so I mean you've got…um you've got more than 24 hours
S hmhm yeah uhuh it would be just a question of ah trying to…get the most from the…from this particular book which um
T I mean this is Thursday and you got it you did get it on Monday did you say?
S no no I got this particular book only yesterday
T you got it yesterday right right
S yeah so yesterday and um I mean if I if I read through it / I mean obviously I don't have to read all of it but the parts that I do have

to read um it would take maybe another couple of days to sort of…you know

T well you you you don't really have a couple of days do you?

S hm

T I mean this is um…it seems to me Pasquale there's a bit of a pattern…

S hmhm

T I mean you you um you are a postgraduate student

S yeah

T you're not an undergraduate you're a you know you're a mature student now um you do have to learn to organise your time I think you you… uh it's not just the lateness with the essays it's…you're you're quite often late to classes / you you miss classes sometimes / you arrived you arrived 20 minutes into my lecture yesterday

S yeah yeah I meant to apologise for that because um I don't know if you know but I've… I work quite late on certain week nights / and you know I've got a part-time job and sometimes you know in the mornings you know it's difficult to get in bang on time I know that was just you know I missed half the lesson so it's a fair… / it's not just ten minutes it was a good half hour / that was that was just a one-off that time I mean that that won't happen normally

T well it has happened a few times…actually

S the full half hour?

T well no no but um arriving late

S hmhm

T it's quite you know…it does disturb the other students

S yeah I can appreciate that / it does yeah it would disturb other students

T who do endeavour to arrive on time

S hmhm hmhm

T you know um so I just…well I …that's not really connected with the essay it's just I thought I ought to mention it because I think that it's important that you…

S yeah

T you know you learn to organise your time better

S I have been meaning to talk to you about that yeah I mean to apologise for the…for the lateness

T yes well it's not really just for me I'm more worried about the other students being disturbed and you not uh not organising yourself because if you um if you want to work in the film industry you know / which you I think you told me you did uh at one point um

S yeah

T you know you're meeting deadlines all the time you you you have to be very

S quite right

T you have to work very fast you have to work…it's stressful you have to work at a very fast pace

S hmhm

T I mean I appreciate that you're…whatever you're doing

S hmhm

T you say you've got a part-time job um…but uh but I still think that you knew that when you started the course

S hmhm

T you you must have known that you would um you would be…maybe needing to work to supplement your

S yeah yeah

T um your funding and so on but um…but you need to you need to work around all these problems

S to manage my time more effectively yeah

T you can't just come to see me and present them as reasons for for handing in an essay late you know

S hm

T you have to…to take responsibility for yourself

S hmhm no I can appreciate that I mean with…you know if I'm thinking of what it's like for the other students if they see a…you know…one student getting two extensions then…

T well

S it doesn't look particularly…good

T well exactly I mean that's why I introduced the ten per cent rule

S hm

T in the first place…um a few years ago because there were…there were students who always handed in their essays on time / they worked really really hard they maybe stayed up all night

S yeah

T they but they got those essays in on time

S hmhm

T other students there were inevitably a few students who would come along and um I would you know maybe be too kind and say 'ok yes you can have another day or two' and then the um the students who had all worked so hard to hand the essays in on time came to me and said you know 'this is not fair'

S yeah

T 'cause these people are getting extra time so they're going to produce um…something better' and I think if I let you have an extension this is exactly what would happen / you would

S yeah I mean it's…

T have time to read the book properly and…

S hmhm

T really absorb it

S hmhm hmhm

T and you know write a better essay undoubtedly than the one you're going to be able to give me tomorrow at five o'clock / but then is that fair on the other students?

S I mean…I quite understand / I mean I was on the other side of…of the fence when I was doing my undergraduate work / I mean I would always hand in hand my essay in on time / I would see other students you know saunter in and you know…

T hmhm hmhm

S two or three days late

T hmhm

S and it does

T so you see my point?

S no I do I do I do see your point yeah / and I do appreciate everything everything you've said um so I think Friday it'll have to be tomorrow then

T yes

S either…

T yes yes yes / yeah I mean if you if you don't give it in tomorrow then I'm not going to…I'm not going to waive the ten per cent rule because

S hmhm

T it really wouldn't be um…it really wouldn't be fair on the other students

S fair on the others right ok

T ok so are you… you're going to manage that aren't you?

S I'll try I'll try my very best you know I'll try my very best to get it done by…by tomorrow as I say I mean it's / I'll try to get the most out of the source you know and then

T yes yes yes well treat it as a…treat it as a learning experience in time management and so on

S no of course yeah yeah exactly

T and you know you may still manage to produce something…

S hopefully yeah fingers crossed

T reasonably good

S yes

T it may not be the best / it may not

S uhuh

T be as good as you want it to be but at least you will have…um you will have done it as you were supposed to / you will have done it in the required time

S hmhm

T along with everybody else / you'll have the same chances as everybody else

S hmhm

T um I mean ok it is annoying that the recalled book took longer to come back but you know…

S it does happen

T you have to factor all these things into your planning you see

S yes so you mean take this sort of thing into account I mean it does happen hmhm

T yes yes there is…you know next time just just plan ahead

S hmhm

T more than you have done and also just try and you know improve the punctuality

S the punctuality as well yeah I know that could be improved yeah

T ok

S um thanks thanks very much

T well I'll have to run now myself so…um but we're we're agreed then?

S yes we're agreed yeah I'll get it in tomorrow you know I'll get it in 5 pm

T right ok that's good ok / bye Pasquale

S thanks very much

Sample 2: Non-native speakers

T = Tutor   (female, Chinese)
S = Student   (male, Portuguese)

S   hi Dr Wu

T   good morning

S   good morning / uh I came to see you because I have a little problem with uh tomorrow's deadline

T   uhuh

S   for the essay uh the question is…since the beginning since I started preparing the assignment the essay I…I always wanted to put some data from my own country to…to turn the essay richer and be more interesting for me as well but there's a problem that the book I needed to to to search…to get information from is…was borrowed and there's only one copy in the library / so it was borrowed a long time ago / I recalled it and uh I could only have access to the book uh…yesterday so as the deadline for the essay…the essay is tomorrow I think it will be impossible for me to to read the book and analyse it and write uh the essay for tomorrow / my guess is that I will need at least two more days um to do that and probably I will only be able to hand in the assignment on Monday

T   how much have you finished?

S   um basically…I only need to put that data / apart from that everything is almost done so…it's only that part

T   hm could you write it more…more quickly? because I'm very busy next week I have no time to mark the essay I think / I want to mark the essay in this weekend / I think it's good to mark all the students' essays together / uh it's fair to other students / if I can't do this work this weekend um the other students can't get their essay back

S   hm yes I understand I understand but…I reckon that I think it will be only possible for me to to to finish the essay on Sunday um…uh maybe I don't know but um…you could mark the whole papers on on the weekend and uh…then you will only have mine to mark

T   yeah

S   on Monday

T   no I couldn't mark it on Monday / I have a I have a meet…I have a meeting at that day

S   uhuh

T   so I think it's better if you hand in your homework before the Sunday

S uhuh

T so I can have some times to mark it

S hmhm

T is it possible?

S um it might be but I think it will be um…um there will be a very low probability because…I need to read the book and I start…I have already started but uh the book is not so simple and um…I think at least I will need to…I will need two more days / Sunday

T you

S Saturday and…

T we have to…

S and finish it on Sunday I could hand / I don't know but

T you see today is Thursday you can read it today tomorrow and you can write it at Saturday yeah? it's ok?

S um maybe yes I think…uhuh maybe…I'll have to work really hard to do that for Sunday…for Saturday yes Saturday

T yes

S you think uh…I only I can only hand in the assignment on Saturday?

T yeah

S it's not possible on Sunday or Monday?

T I think it's not possible

S uh…all right I'll…do my best I'll try to to hand it…

T ok

S hand in on Saturday / will you be around in the university?

T yes I will be in my office at Saturday afternoon so you can hand it to my office

S hmhm all right hmhm I'll try / thank you very much

T bye

S bye

Comments on the two performances

When discussing the two recordings with our students, we use the feedback framework from page 142, as shown below.

STRATEGY	*Did they manage to get what they wanted?*
	Did one player come away the loser?
INFORMATION	*Did they use relevant role information provided?*
	Did they forget or change any details?
COMMUNICATION	*Were there any breakdowns in communication?*
	How (and how well) did they resolve them?
LANGUAGE	*Did their performance reveal any significant gaps in grammar, vocabulary or pronunciation?*

Strategy

The Portuguese student succeeded in persuading the Chinese tutor to give him an extension until Saturday afternoon. The English tutor did not allow the Scottish student an extension. In this overall sense, we could say that the Scottish student was less successful than the other three players, since he did not get what he wanted; the other three achieved an outcome that suited them.

Information

It is noticeable that the two tutors used their role information in different ways. The English tutor took the opportunity to highlight her student's poor punctuality, as well as criticising his poor time management. The Chinese tutor focused on her own problem – the fact that she needed to get all the essays marked over the weekend because of her involvement in next week's conference. Both tutors 'added' to the information in the same way, by bringing in the issue of fairness to the other students.

Communication

Both performances went smoothly from the communicative point of view and are good examples of effective interaction. There were no points where any of the players had difficulty understanding their interlocutor. You may have noticed a difference in conversational pattern at the start of the two performances. The Portuguese student explained his problem in a relatively long speaking turn, while the tutor listened quietly. We have found this to be quite a common pattern among our students. On the other hand, the British pair's interaction involves more 'give and take' with shorter turns, mainly because the English tutor provided regular back-channelling (signals of understanding and sympathy) – *hmhm, that's right, oh dear, uhuh, I see* and so on.

Language

There are obviously lots of points that one could draw to students' attention. We tend to ask our students to tell us what they have noticed in the transcripts or what they want to ask about. Among the points that have come up in our classes are the following.

1 Which is the correct preposition after *fair*?
   a) English tutor   '*is that fair <u>on</u> the other students?*'
   b) Chinese tutor   '*it's fair <u>to</u> the other students*'

We say that both are used in Britain.

2 The Scottish student says '*I'll try my very best*' (compared with the Portuguese student's '*I'll do my best*'). Our students have asked if the combination VERY + SUPERLATIVE is correct; they assumed it was a mistake. This has led on to discussion of what sort of adjective can be combined with *very*:

very worst, very first, very last	seem acceptable
very smoothest, very purest	limited to adverts (?)
very most beautiful, very tallest	unacceptable.

What do you think?

3 We have been asked about the Portuguese student's expression '*there will be a very low probability*' (when he is asked whether he can get the essay in before Sunday). This seems rather formal. We would say '*I don't think I can*' or '*I don't think there's much chance of that*', and we would probably add a softener like '*I'm afraid*'.

4 There are of course various natural slips in both sets of performances, which are entirely normal in unscripted conversation. The English tutor says '*bought*' instead of '*brought*' (and then corrects herself). The Chinese tutor says she needs '*some times*' to mark the essays, when she means '*time*'. We point these out to underline the fact that both native and non-native speakers make this sort of slip.

References

Anderson, K. and Lynch, T. (1996) *PROFILE – Principles, Resources and Options for the Independent Learner of English*. Edinburgh: Institute for Applied Language Studies, University of Edinburgh.

Bygate, M. (1988) Units of oral expression and language learning in small group interaction. *Applied Linguistics*. 9/1: 59–82.

Canale, M. and Swain, M. (1980) Theoretical bases of communicative approaches to second language teaching and testing. *Applied Linguistics*. 1/1: 1–47.

Coxhead, A. (2000) A new academic word list. *TESOL Quarterly*. 34/2: 213–38.

Dalton, C. and Seidlhofer, B. (1994) *Pronunciation*. Oxford: Oxford University Press.

Di Pietro, R. (1987) *Strategic Interaction*. Cambridge: Cambridge University Press.

Duff, P. (1986) Another look at interlanguage talk: taking task to task. In R.R. Day (ed.) *Talking to Learn: Conversation in Second Language Acquisition*. Rowley, Mass: Newbury House.

Faerch, C. and Kasper, C. (1986) The role of comprehension in second language learning. *Applied Linguistics*. 7/3: 257–74.

Jenkins, J. (2000) *The Phonology of English as an International Language*. Oxford: Oxford University Press.

Krashen, S. (1981) *Second Language Acquisition and Second Language Learning*. Oxford: Pergamon.

Luk, V. (1994) Developing Interactional Listening Strategies in a Foreign Language: A Study of Two Classroom Approaches. Unpublished PhD thesis, University of Edinburgh.

Lynch, T. (2001a) Seeing what they meant: transcribing as a route to noticing. *ELT Journal*. 55/2: 124–32.

Lynch, T. (2001b) Promoting EAP learner autonomy in a second language university context. In J. Flowerdew and M. Peacock (eds) *Research Perspectives in English for Academic Purposes*. Cambridge: Cambridge University Press.

Lynch, T. and Anderson, K. (1991) 'Do you mind if I come in here?' – a comparison of EAP materials and real seminars. In P. Adams, B. Heaton and P. Howarth (eds) *Socio-cultural Issues in English for Academic Purposes*. London: Macmillan ELT.

Lynch, T. and Anderson, K. (2003) Learner/non-teacher interactions: the contribution of a course assistant to EAP speaking classes. In J. Burton and C. Clennell (eds) *Interaction and Language Learning*. Alexandria, VA: TESOL.

Lynch. T. and Maclean, J. (2001) 'A case of exercising': Effects of immediate task repetition on learners' performance. In M. Bygate, P. Skehan and M. Swain (eds) *Researching Pedagogic Tasks: Second Language Learning, Teaching and Testing*. Harlow: Longman.

Maurice, K. (1983) The fluency workshop. *TESOL Newsletter*. 17: 29.

Rutherford, W. (1987) *Second Language Grammar*. Harlow: Longman.

Seedhouse, P. (1999) Task-based interaction. *ELT Journal*. 53/3: 149–56.

Sharwood Smith, M. (1981) Consciousness-raising and the second language learner. *Applied Linguistics*. 2/2: 159–68.

Swain, M. (1985) Communicative competence: some roles of comprehensive input and comprehensible output in its development. In S. Gass and C. Madden (eds) *Input in Second Language Acquisition*. Rowley, Mass: Newbury House.

Tarone, E. and Yule, G. (1989) *Focus on the Language Learner*. Oxford: Oxford University Press.